WRITE IT RIGHT

A Manual for Writing Family Histories and Genealogies

by
Donald R. Barnes, C.G.
and
Richard S. Lackey, C.G.
Fellow, American Society of Genealogists

Introduction by
John Frederick Dorman, C.G.
Fellow, American Society of Genealogists

19 83

Lyon Press
Ocala, Florida

First Edition
Published in 1983 by Lyon Press

Second Edition 1988

ORDER FROM:

D.R. Barnes Associates
Box 5755
Rockville, Maryland 20855-0755
Price: $7.95

Add $1.00 for postage and handling.
(Maryland residents add 5% sales tax)

Library of Congress Catalog Card Number:
83-90241

Printed and bound in the
United States of America

Set in type by Ellen Lackey

Richard Stephen Lackey

1941-1983

FOREWORD

Write It Right has been written as a companion volume to Cite Your Sources. It provides genealogists with a clear and easily understood guide for writing a family history or genealogy article or book.

Advice is given to writers about confronting such problems as adoptees, skeletons, coats of arms, conflicting evidence, among many others.

All genealogists, professional or amateur, will benefit from this book. The authors literally take you by the hand and lead you every step of the way in writing your article or book.

This book was written in response to suggestions made by many persons at various seminars, workshops, and lectures. Additionally, Richard Lackey and I had innumerable discussions during the past year and we both had realized for many years the need for such a book. The advice, criticism and suggestions from which we have bene-fited are greatly appreciated, and we wish to take this opportunity to thank the following persons: John Frederick Dorman, C.G., F.A.S.G.; Patricia Downes; our wives, June and Saralyn; and especially Ellen Lackey. Thanks

are also due to Robert Charles
Anderson, C.G., F.A.S.G.; Neil D.
Thompson, C.G., F.A.S.G.; Edward W.
Hanson, Charles M. Hansen, George Ely
Russell, C.G., F.A.S.G., and Robert
Crandall.

Additionally, it is appropriate to
thank the following organizations and
journals for graciously allowing us to
use material from their publications:
The New England Historic Genealogical
Society, The National Genealogical
Society, The Filson Club, The Virginia
Genealogist, The Prince George's
County, Maryland, Genealogical Society,
and The Genealogist.

Finally, a special thanks to my
good friend and co-author, Richard
Lackey, whose friendship and assistance
will always be remembered and valued.

                    Donald Ray Barnes, C.G.

Rockville, Maryland
5 March 1983

INTRODUCTION

The gathering of data through correspondence and research in libraries, court houses, archival institutions and cemeteries is but the beginning of the odyssey of the dedicated genealogist. There are obvious pleasures and rewards to be derived from research but it is the sharing of one's findings with others which constitutes the real joy of genealogy.

This joy of sharing through the compiling of data and the writing of an article or book, however, requires that the genealogist learn how to present the data amassed over the years in a clearly understood format. Unless the finished product--the written article or book--meets certain standards which have been developed through the experience of genealogists over more than a century, the work may be of interest to the writer and those closely related to him, but it will not have the value which the years of research, the expenditure of a significant amount of money and much personal effort demand.

In <u>Write It Right</u>, Donald Barnes and the late Richard Lackey have outlined the steps to be followed to produce a properly written article or book. They begin by explaining how to overcome the natural fears of those who have not before developed experience in writing and step by step lead the novice to the completion of a genealogy, pointing out the pitfalls to be avoided and the generally recognized forms to be followed, often giving examples of poorly presented material and contrasting them with properly expressed and documented accounts.

Although many splendid guides to assist genealogists in their research have been published and a number of manuals designed to assist genealogists in publishing have been issued in recent years, none has before this concentrated on how to write. This intervening step between research and publishing has been a stumbling-block for many genealogists who have seen writing as an impossible task. As a result these genealogists have at their deaths left a mass of unorganized papers which often have been thrown away by heirs who could not understand their contents or, when preserved in an archival institution, have been of minimal value to others because there was no order to the collection.

Only when a genealogist explains in writing the evidence which has been gathered regarding a difficult problem can those who follow have the benefit of the years of experience and study devoted to a resolution of the problem. By failing to write, too many genealogists of the past have forced those who have come after them to reinvent the wheel. The authors have recognized the necessity of encouraging proper genealogical writing and through study of this book it should be possible for every genealogist to produce written accounts which will stand for years to come as authoritative presentations about the families chosen for discussion.

Write It Right fills a gap in the ever increasing list of genealogical manuals. It is a milestone in genealogical bibliography.

John Frederick Dorman, Fellow
American Society of Genealogists

Washington, D.C.
7 March 1983

CONTENTS

Chapter V: WRITING THE TEXT

Chapter VI: THE FINAL DRAFT

Chapter VII: PROBLEMS AND ADVICE

Chapter VIII: CITATIONS AND BIBLIOGRAPHY

Chapter IX: MECHANICS

APPENDIX A

APPENDIX B

APPENDIX C

Chapter I

PREPARING TO WRITE

WRITE IT RIGHT

At some stage, every genealogist should stop doing research, compile his notes and write, and should, by all means--*WRITE IT RIGHT!* Obviously, you agree and have purchased this book. We will attempt to show you in the succeeding chapters many important things we have learned about writing. Writing your genealogy or family history is an excellent end result of all those countless hours you have spent on research. To share is the greatest gift we have!

THE SUBJECT

What shall be your subject? As a genealogist you look around and see copies of documents and research notes. Your file cabinet is overflowing--papers are stacked on the desk--documents fill boxes on the floor. You need never worry what your subject will be! Never worry, because it is there before you in the file cabinets--on the desk--and on the floor. The subject of your research will be the subject of your book or article! You simply need to transfer the facts from those copies of documents and research notes onto paper and into a compiled genealogy. This manual will show you how to do that step by step.

It is not necessary for you to have advanced formal education or a great deal of experience in writing. What is necessary is that you have an insatiable desire to share your work with others and that you follow some acceptable standards. Any person who recognizes these standards and has the desire to write can do so.

ARE WRITERS BORN OR TAUGHT?

We are not training you to be a William Faulkner or a William Shakespeare. Our purpose is to introduce genealogical writing in such a manner that anyone who can conduct successful and competent research can present that research in a compiled genealogy acceptable to scholars in the field. Any person can be taught to write a grammatically correct sentence. Your genealogical writing must be as grammatically correct as possible. The same is true for punctuation and spelling. Anyone needing help with these areas can obtain assistance through many different available sources.

Writing a compiled genealogy requires special knowledge and skill that set it apart from other work in the field of genealogy. Record abstracts, source material compilations, indices, bibliographies, "how-to" books, and articles are all valuable studies. However, it is not necessary for a writer/compiler to be a genealogist to produce most of these works. On the other hand, it is *absolutely* essential that a writer of a compiled genealogy be a genealogist. The more skilled you are as a genealogist, the more useful this manual will be. *The things that distinguish a genealogist from a researcher--the ability to evaluate, interpret and analyze documents, the ability to place individuals and families in proper historical perspective, and the ability to employ "genealogical reasoning"--are all necessary skills you will need in order to write a compiled genealogy. Like grammar, spelling, and punctuation, these skills are learned and are not innate.*

Style is individual and is part of the character of the writer. It is the combination of the writer's collective experience and perception of how one fact relates to another. Many persons do not realize their own style until they start to write. It is only then, when you allow your mind to guide your

3

hand, that you see your style develop. This is a tremendous experience and you can do it if you will follow these steps!

You, the writer, whatever your subject, have now come to the point where it is time to use all your acquired skills to bring your subjects alive by writing about them. It is time to lift them from the pages of your forgotten family history and to imbue them, for all time, with your breath of life. Strip all dullness from the documents and the research notes and generate excitement. Only you have a feel for your ancestors or the subject of your writing. Project yourself into their time; re-live the Battle of Gettysburg. Make your readers know "Little Granny," "Mimi," "Cow John," or "Aunt Georgia" and "Uncle Arkansas." Scholarly writing does not prevent you from being realistic. For example, if your great-grandfather said that after the War Between the States the family was "Po(or)as Job's Turkey," do not indicate that he said the family "lost its position of affluence."

If you do nothing more than present the facts as you found them, you can miss the most intriguing part of the story. Writing an interesting compiled genealogy involves more than photocopying pages of documents at the archives, receiving charts and letters from your relatives, setting the pages in type, and publishing the material "the way you got it." Writing a successful compiled genealogy involves careful selection and analysis of facts that in many cases are held together by nothing more than your own assumptions gleaned from the related facts, if only by inference.

You are writing about real people and how they felt, loved, lived, and died. You are recording the facts about their lives for all time. Indeed, you are lifting them from the pages of your forgotten family history. Your efforts are not just for you but are for all of the generations who follow. Look for the human qualities in your ancestors. Were they stubborn, talkative, inventive, practical, self-reliant, loving, religious? You may project your readers into the seventeenth century to a colonial farm. You may get such a feel for these persons that, if you were an artist, it would be possible to commit them to canvas. Not all of us are painters, but readers may conjure up mental images from your writing about these persons.

Your writing will be a reflection of you. Prepare to do the very best you can, and the rewards will be limitless. You have a knowledge of your subject, you have acquired the necessary skills, and you should not be afraid to inject your thoughts or style into your writing. The only exception is when you must conform your style to the request of an editor or publisher. The best way to learn is by doing. The first sentence will be the hardest, just as your first article or book will be the hardest. After you write for a while, it becomes easier to achieve clarity of expression.

SOLID RESEARCH

The best genealogies are based on solid research. Good genealogists do not rely only on facts that come to light easily. Indeed not! Good genealogists know available records and search for needed information. Before writing you should do your research at as many facilities as possible. Exhaust these facilities. Leave no stone unturned. The more information you have assembled on your subject, the greater the degree of an accurate interpretation.

Quantity of information is, however, no substitute for quality. The best standard of proof is based on the quality of the source. Primary evidence in original form provides the writer with the best possible proof for statements of fact. Facts founded on this type of source provide an excellent base for reasonable conclusions after consideration of all evidence.

Always remember that genealogists do not settle for half the answers. We want all the answers possible. Go the extra mile; find the additional evidence you need. Undoubtedly there will be many occasions when you do not find all the evidence you need, and you must remember that genealogy is a lot of conjecture developed by weighing the evidence at hand. Certainly, conjecture must be based on the preponderance of all the available evidence to reach a valid conclusion. We agree with the well-known genealogist, Dr. Neil D. Thompson, C.G., F.A.S.G., who often says, "One of the best ways to see where you stand with your research is to write." Be sure your writing is based on solid research.

NEED FOR COMPILING A GENEALOGY

Your writing can add something of value to present knowledge or can correct errors. You are probably an authority on the subject of your research. Possibly no other person has amassed an equal amount of material on your subject. Further, no person may ever live again who will have the inclination, time, or opportunity to do the research you have done. You must preserve this knowledge you have gained

7

as the result of years of research, and you must start compiling your genealogy. Do you not feel a compulsive urge to write your own genealogy? Too much genealogical information has been lost to trash collectors because (now deceased) genealogists never found the time to compile their work. Are you going to risk letting your collection go in the trash? You might not be able to prevent that, but if you compile and publish the results of your research, then a part of you and your work will be preserved forever. Get busy now--it is later than you think!

BE PRACTICAL

Start with a short article. You will realistically be able to reach your goal, you will build needed confidence, and you will learn a lot about writing. Do not plan a ten volume set as your first writing project. On your first attempt at writing a compiled genealogy, do not even plan a book. A short article on one subject is a reasonable point of beginning. The shorter it is, the better.

Set a future date to finish your writing project. Be realistic, and allow enough time to complete your work. Most genealogists have church, family, job, community, and other responsibilities. With only twenty-four hours in a day, usually a limited amount of time can be spent writing. Work toward a definite target date to finish.

ENJOY IT

A real pleasure comes to those who write. The pleasure is not just seeing your finished work but in doing the writing. Most genealogists have experienced the personal satisfaction of doing research. If you have not been writing, you are in for an additional treat. Sit with all the documents and notes organized for quick reference, the facts relating to your family cataloged in your brain, ready to be retrieved, pencil in hand and a blank sheet of paper before you. Your thoughts will guide your hand and the words will flow onto the paper page by page--then re-write and re-read until every sentence conveys your thoughts. Take pure pleasure in simply recording the past in your own words! Yes, writing is fun, so enjoy it.

Chapter II

PURPOSE

A MUST FOR WRITERS

Great advantages accrue to the writer when he states a purpose before any further thought is given to writing. A composition written in accordance with a specific purpose will have unity, cohesiveness, and clarity. If every phase of writing is done with the overall purpose in the writer's mind, the composition will have continuity. From the outset you know where you are going when you have a purpose. While stating the purpose will not insure success of a project, experts in every field agree that an understanding of one's purpose in any action is always a necessary step. Genealogists are certainly no exception! Every genealogist who contemplates writing should have as his cardinal rule: STATE YOUR PURPOSE!

One great advantage to the writer's stating his purpose is that the purpose itself will set parameters for the composition. Almost every genealogist has far more material than can ever be utilized in one book or article. A purpose will allow the genealogist a better basis on which to select that material which relates to the project at hand.

THE EMPHASIS OF YOUR WORK

Genealogists are not writing novels. Certainly you are not writing fiction. Exactly what is the nature of your work? It is necessary prior to stating their purpose for most researchers to consider that most compiled genealogies can be classified as (1) biographical, (2) historical, or (3) analytical. Certainly any work could also be a balanced combination of any two or all three.

The vast majority of compiled genealogies are biographical in nature. Organization of facts presented about an individual is usually chronological, and emphasis is determined by how the writer views events in a subject's life using available records. The subject is identified by all or as much as possible of the following information: full name, date and place of birth, date and place of death, and relatives. Once an individual is identified in this manner, other events in his life can be discussed, and it can be demonstrated that the individual mentioned in any given record is reasonably identified as the subject. The writer would usually follow identity with facts which disclose activities in the person's life: education, marriage, military service, occupation, migrations, children, and other events and activities.

A more intriguing compiled genealogy could be described as biographical-historical in nature. In such a work, the writer attempts to relate ways in which local, regional, or national events affected or applied to a family, or how the family affected the events. This requires special knowledge and training and should not be attempted by writers lacking either.

Another element which should be incorporated into genealogical writing is analytical in nature. In an analytical work, research problems and potential solutions are central issues. The genealogical researcher/writer is certainly in the best position to analyze properly the status of his research. Of course, a certain amount of analysis is necessary for one to write even one sentence of a genealogy, but analysis cannot be overemphasized as a major portion of any work.

CHOOSE YOUR PURPOSE

Every genealogist realizes that, whatever the nature of the work planned, not all genealogical studies are exactly alike, and it is usually the writer's purpose that makes them different. Some purposes that come to mind are to (1) trace the descendants of a person (or couple) in all lines to the present generation or for any pre-selected number of generations; (2) trace the descendants of a person (or couple) in some lines to the present generation or for any preselected number of generations; (3) trace the ancestry of a person in all lines; (4) trace the ancestry of a person in a single line; (5) establish an immigrant's parentage and/or place of birth; (6) extend a previously published lineage; (7) correct some previously published error; (8) conduct a multi-family project; and (9) others.

EXAMPLES OF DIFFERENT PURPOSES FOR GENEALOGICAL WRITING

1. TRACE THE DESCENDANTS OF A PERSON (OR COUPLE) IN ALL LINES TO THE PRESENT GENERATION OR FOR ANY PRESELECTED NUMBER OF GENERATIONS.

This is the most ambitious of all genealogical projects. Most would agree that it would be unlikely to think that anyone COULD TRACE ALL the descendants of an American colonist to the present generations. To think of all the different surnames and the number of individuals that one would reasonably encounter boggles the mind!

A difficult, but far more practical, project would be to trace all of the descendants of a person or couple in all lines for, say, three or four generations. The Board for Certification of Genealogists requires applicants for certification as a Certified Genealogist to submit a genealogy "of descendants of a couple through three generations, listing the children in the fourth generation,..." Applicants are told, in addition to other instructions, that "females should be included and all children, including those who died in infancy should be listed." Could you not trace all the descendants in all lines of one set of great-grandparents? Think of how valuable such a record would become to both present and future generations.

2. TRACE THE DESCENDANTS OF A PERSON (OR COUPLE) IN SOME LINES TO THE PRESENT GENERATION OR FOR ANY PRESELECTED NUMBER OF GENERATIONS.

Most genealogists recognize that circumstances, such as the loss of necessary records, sometimes make it impractical to attempt to carry all lines of some families three or four generations. This is especially true if the first generation lived in America during the colonial period. For an individual writer who is not making an application for certification

14

with the Board for Certification of
Genealogists or doing work for a client
with instructions to the contrary, lack
of interest in tracing collateral lines
may be reason enough to restrict the
purpose of a writing project to tracing
descendants in one single or in certain
lines. We, as genealogists, most often
choose to write about the earliest
generation of our proved or probable
ancestry. This is definitely important, for it records our research
results permanently, and often we have
spent years working on it. Further, it
aids all the researchers who will
follow, as others can build on our
efforts. These family studies ideally
should cover the first four generations
and should try to document the lives of
the early generations.

3. TRACE THE ANCESTRY IN ALL LINES OF A
PERSON.

For some reason, people place great
emphasis on their own surname. One
would think some beginning genealogists
had only a "paternal line!" All of the
individuals in your ancestry are
important and interesting, and it can
be a rewarding project to write about
your ancestry in all lines.

4. TRACE THE ANCESTRY OF A PERSON IN A
SINGLE LINE.

There may be some reason you would wish to restrict a writing project to the single line of ancestry of a person. For example, you may have one line of ancestry that is more interesting to you than any other line. If so, write about only that line if you wish that to be your purpose. Many genealogists like to write about the line of their ancestry that they found most difficult to prove. This is tremendous! Think of the time you will save other researchers, and, too, the world can see how you solved it.

5. ESTABLISH AN IMMIGRANT'S PARENTAGE AND/OR PLACE OF BIRTH.

If the earliest ancestor was also the proved immigrant, we need to utilize as many sources as possible in trying to document his/her place and point of origin. All too often we are confused by the obvious, *i.e.*, just because the ship carrying our ancestor left from Cowes, such a fact would not necessarily imply an English origin for an ancestor. After all, that ship may well have originally sailed from Le Havre. All immigrants should be researched thoroughly on this side of the Atlantic before we make quantum leaps across the ocean. Sadly, we are often guilty of appropriating ancestry, as we call it. This is the process

whereby we connect our proved ancestors
to those of families in England,
Ireland, France, Germany, *etc.* of the
same surname, without fully documenting
the connection. In too many instances,
the only research that has been com-
pleted involves a similarity of surname, at best. Many genealogies have a
chapter on an ancient family that
flourished in England in the sixteenth
century. This is followed by a chapter
on the proved ancestor of the same
surname who was born in America in
1805. The implication, if not the
claim, is that the ancestor was a
descendant of the flourishing ancient
English family of that name. This
serves no purpose and should be
avoided. Why spend your time attempting
to trace wrong lineages? It does not
matter whether the ancestors are yours
or a client's. Do it right, and always
remember that an error doubles each
generation! In ten generations, there
would be 1,024 ancestors in error. All
of this could be avoided by documenting
each generation carefully.

6. EXTEND A PREVIOUSLY PUBLISHED
LINEAGE.

No genealogical work is ever complete,
and this is what makes genealogy ever-
interesting and always fascinating. We
should attempt to add to the work of
others. You are indeed fortunate if

you find good material previously published about your family. Whenever you
can, extend the lineage or add to the
published information. It is not
necessary to "rehash" what is presently
in print if it is accurate. If you do
plan to publish material that has been
previously published, plan to do it
better by adding considerable and significant information such as an every
name index. There should not be any
reward, and there usually is not, for
appropriating the work of another. It
is most rewarding to add something of
value to the present knowledge in the
field.

7. CORRECT SOME PREVIOUSLY PUBLISHED
ERROR.

Correct errors with courtesy. Remember
that the next error that needs
correcting may be yours. This is not
to say that correction of errors should
not be made firmly--they should be made
firmly and clearly, but without
insults. Fraud or the work of char-
latans is a different matter, and such
published rubbish should be "exposed"
and not "corrected." More often than
we would like, it is necessary to
"correct" the work of a well-meaning,
but unqualified, researcher and writer.
This is a difficult and sometime
delicate matter, especially if no harm
or fraud was intended. For too long,

purchasers of genealogies have taken the attitude, "anything in print is better than nothing." This is simply not so. Errors, untruths, and, yes-- fabricated lines--once published, are very, very difficult to overcome. There seems to be a current theory that, if something is published enough times, it assumes unquestioned author- ity. Genealogists must never feel this way. As we work with the original records, it is our duty to correct and publish new information as we find it. Correcting previously published material may enable other researchers and those who follow to find earlier generations. This is one of the distinct rewards of genealogical writing.

8. CONDUCT A MULTI-FAMILY PROJECT.

An interesting project could be the study of several neighboring families, known to be related, who moved from one place to another. The migration of families from St. Mary's County, Maryland, to Pottinger's Creek, Nelson County, Kentucky, beginning in 1785, could be such a project. A writer might show how the families were interrelated, why they moved as a group, and other such information.

9. OTHER.

Legends add to your family lore and
heritage, but they must be proved.
Just think, you may be the first person
to prove or disprove a legend in your
family and learn the truth. You should
try to document the facts and, at last,
to write the accurate account. Your
reward will remain with you for all
time. One hundred years from now, your
great-grandchildren will read your
article. Not only will the ancestor
you wrote about step off the stage of
history, but you will also seem alive
to your descendants. Imagine the continuity in family tradition when they
ask their parents about you, and their
parents relate stories about grand-
mother or grandfather, who wrote the
family history. Naturally the icing on
the cake comes when these persons (our
descendants) tell their grandchildren
that their great-grandparents actually
remembered these relatives. The generations fall into place, and suddenly
we are face to face with two hundred
years of history and ancestry. What
happened over two hundred years ago
will seem like yesterday. Indeed,
there is no generation gap in
genealogy!

Many of us discover descent from a
colonial doctor, lawyer, clergyman,
etc. and decide to document his life.
We may even decide to research all the
colonial doctors in Maryland, for

instance, or all the lawyers of Virginia for a certain time period. Again, articles and books of this type would require us to become familiar with the court, medical, religious, and political system of any given period of time. Knowledge of specific disciplines opens entire record collections that might otherwise be overlooked. Not only do we become better genealogists, but we have additional material to assist us in bringing our ancestors alive.

Obviously, the examples above are of a general nature, and writers should decide on their own purposes after considering many factors. Once the purpose of a project is determined, other work can proceed. We hope, however, you see the importance of stating your purpose at a very early stage in writing.

LIMITATIONS

Are genealogists free to state a purpose in any manner desired? With the exception of the professional genealogist working within the limits set by a client and those completing work for a class or for some professional certifying or accrediting group, most writers of genealogical material enjoy a remarkable freedom to state their purposes as they desire. Very few genealogists are under contract with editors or publishers before the actual writing begins. Quite the contrary; most genealogical articles and books are written and then submitted to editors and publishers for possible publication. When no outside party is paying the fiddler, the fiddler calls his own tunes. This freedom to select and pursue his chosen purpose can be a great advantage to the writer and can help make writing a real joy.

READER AUDIENCE

Because of the very nature of the subject, genealogically related works have limited appeal to commercial publishers. The possible or potential audience of readers of their compositions should be considered carefully by writers.

POTENTIAL READER AUDIENCE FOR GENEALOGIES

1. Non-genealogists interesed only in books/articles about their own ancestors or relatives.
2. Genealogists interested only in books/articles about their own ancestors or relatives.
3. Genealogists with a wide range of interests in well written or interesting books/articles on any family.

4. Genealogists, especially professionals, interested in any books/articles which make a valuable contribution to the literature in the field.
5. Genealogical educators seeking needed written material for classroom work.
6. Scholars and readers in related fields.

The importance of audience identification will, to some extent, dictate the writer's final plans. Does the writer plan to market the composition or present it as a gift? Obviously, an article or book that has a potentially large audience will probably enjoy the most success in the marketplace. Genealogists are fortunate to have numerous scholarly publications whose editors are willing to publish, at no cost to the writer, articles that make a valuable contribution to the literature in the field. Few, if any, commercial publishers will risk publishing genealogical material with very limited appeal, and the writer or a sponsor is usually required to bear all the cost of publication.

In order to attract a larger audience, it is sometimes possible and usually wise to keep the purpose as broad as possible. For example, identification of particular immigrants, or, as genealogist Timothy Field Beard,

F.A.S.G., calls them, "gateway
ancestors", might be of limited interest. But such a work could be expanded
to become a methodology or source composition. In this way, it would capture the attention of readers interested in that particular family, immigrants in general, and in methods and
sources used in proving immigrants.
Experienced writers will find that they
can often attract wide reader interest
by expanding the potential reader
audience for a work.

Chapter III

NUMBERING SYSTEMS

POINTS TO CONSIDER

It is imperative for a writer to select one numbering system at this point in the writing project. A numbering system adds clarity to any compiled genealogy. When each person in a family is identified by an individual number, the identity of that person is always clear to the reader no matter when or where the name of that person along with the identifying number appears in the composition. This is quite helpful when you have several different people with the same given name and the same surname. With a clear numbering system, the reader--or, for that matter, the writer--is never asking, "Which John is this?" Always be consistent with the system used.

There is no "single" numbering system that must be used in writing a compiled genealogy. System after system has been devised to assign individual numbers (or letters or combinations of numbers and letters) to individual family members. It seems that some genealogical writers feel obligated to develop their own unique

system. Have you spent hours inter-
preting some of these unique "individual systems," such as
"3Ab(13)BB462d4?" Do you know the type
we mean? There is no reason to feel
that you have to devise your own
system. A numbering format should aid
the writer and the reader and should
never complicate the work of either.

The most important point to
remember is that no matter what system
you select, whether it is one you
devise or one you "borrow" from someone
else, you must be sure that you fully
understand the system you select.
Further, be certain you explain the
system to the reader, either in a note
or in your introduction. You should
not expect even a knowledgable reader
to find that any system is easy to
understand unless you select one of the
widely used systems. The systems
recommended in this manual are understood by most active genealogists
today.

The numbering system provides you
with a format for your book or article.
Many researchers who have no knowledge
or conception of any numbering system
do realize that their genealogical
writing must have some format, and they
attempt to use the "outline" format.
Because of the necessity of indenting,
soon the writer is using only about
twenty per cent of the paper. This is

disadvantage enough without mentioning the problems that come with attempting to follow Arabic and Roman numbers and upper and lower case letters after several generations. The outline format is not necessary when a proper numbering system is used, and it is not recommended for a genealogy.

There is no single "correct" numbering system that writers are obligated to follow. Over a long period, three systems have emerged as most favored by recognized genealogists, especially by well-known editors of leading periodicals. Modified forms of these are often recommended, and are sometimes required, by some editors and publishers. The Register System (used in the New England Historical and Genealogical Register), the Henry System, and the Sosa-Stradonitz System are all recommended.

DESCENDANTS OR ANCESTORS?

As stated earlier, writing a compiled genealogy involves a step-by-step process. As soon as you decide on your purpose, then decide on your numbering system so you will have a format to follow. Of the three systems (the Register System, the Henry System, and the Sosa-Stradonitz System), the purpose of your writing will almost determine the system you select.

After you have written your purpose, look at it and ask yourself this question: "Does this involve descendants or ancestors?" If your answer is "descendants" then you will probably want to use the Register System or the Henry System. If your answer is "ancestors" you will probably want to use the Sosa-Stradonitz System. You will soon learn that either the Register System or the Henry System lends itself to both descendants and ancestor in one line of descent. The Sosa-Stradonitz System is unusable if you plan to carry descendants in multiple lines through several genera-tions. The Sosa-Stradonitz System is the best when it is the writer's purpose to record all or more than one line in a person's ancestry. Notice that the Register System and the Henry System begin with the earliest known progenitor and come forward. Also, notice that the Sosa-Stradonitz System begins with a descendant and goes back.

THE REGISTER SYSTEM

The Register System or a modified form usually meets the needs of most writers of genealogy. It provides an excellent format by which to arrange information and number individuals. An Arabic number is used to identify only

28

those individuals to be fully discussed later. This system is strictly observed in The New England Historical and Genealogical Register. The earliest progenitor being discussed shall be individual number 1 (one). For example, in the Gay genealogy below, David Gay is assigned number 1. His seventh child, Lewis Gay, would be number 8. Following a narrative on Lewis Gay, the writer provided a listing of his children. Note that the writer indents and then lists his children in columnar form in order of their birth, including those that died in infancy. Small Roman numerals should be used to indicate the order of birth. Number all children consecutively (with small Roman numerals) even if a child left no descendants. When a person has more than one wife (or husband), this should be indicated, and the children by each wife or husband should be presented in separate lists. Study the example below which was published in N.G.S.Q., Vol. 67, No. 2 (June 1979) pp. 85-97. The system is simple to understand once it is studied and used. Try it!

EXAMPLE 1

8. LEWIS[6] GAY was born at Onslow, Nova Scotia, 23 December 1780, son of David and Thankful (Hayward) Gay, and died in or near Zanesville, Ohio, 28

February 1845. He married first 24 September 1811, ELIZABETH TAPPING, who died 28 November 1818. Lewis married , second, 15 August 1820, MARY LANE, who died 29 March 1860.[53]

Lewis Gay moved to Ohio to complete the process of disposing of his father's Refugee land, a process begun by his brother Lemuel. At the 1830 Federal census he was residing in Muskingum Township, Muskingum County, Ohio.[54]
Children of Lewis and Elizabeth (Tapping) Gay:

31   i. Vixen Pyrhus[7] Gay, b. 31 July 1814.
32   ii. (daughter), b. 31 July 1814; d. young.
33 iii. Volney E. Gay, b. 9 Jan. 1817.

Child of Lewis and Mary (Lane) Gay:
34   iv. Garoa G. Gay, b. 18 Aug. 1821.

Robert Charles Anderson, C.G., F.A.S.G., "David Gay (1739-ca. 1815) of Onslow, Nova Scotia, and Lincolnville, Maine,"The National Genealogical Society Quarterly, Vol. 67, No. 2 (June 1979) p. 94.

Note: References given at end of article.

MODIFIED REGISTER SYSTEM

An individual Arabic number, assigned consecutively, will be used to identify each person in the genealogy. This modified form allows use of an Arabic number assignment to each individual. The earliest progenitor being discussed shall be individual number 1 (one). For example, a ......genealogy may begin with the earliest known ancestor, ..., as in the example below.

The writer would provide a heading such as one of the following:

Issue of John Smith, wife Mary Jones

Children of John Smith and his wife Mary ?

Issue of John Smith, wife unknown

The writer would then indent ten spaces and list his children in columnar form in order of their birth, including those that died in infancy. Small Roman numerals should be used to indicate the order of birth. Number all children consecutively even if a child left no descendants. When a person has more than one wife (or husband), this should be indicated, and the children by each wife or husband should be presented in separate lists.

31

The sign "+" in front of a name indicates that more information will be presented as an organized family unit in a later portion of the genealogy. The "+" sign is unnecessary if only those individuals being fully treated are given Arabic numbers, as is the case with the strict use of the Register System. But, in the modified form where all descendants are assigned an Arabic number, the "+" is needed. Brief statements of identity should be presented about persons following their names in a columnar list. If extensive information is to be presented and descendants in the line continued later, the sign "+" should appear in front of the name, and the information would be organized as a separate family unit in a later section. For example, a standard format for a manuscript might appear:

EXAMPLE 2

12. BENJAMIN^4 HURD (Benjamin^3, Jacob^2, John^1) was baptized on 8 February 1718/9. He was a leather dresser and resided in Charlestown, where he died on 30 July 1808, age 90. He married, first, 25 December 1744, HANNAH RAND, who died on 30 October 1747, age 21. On 11 October 1748, he married GRACE EASTERBROOK, who died on 26 December 1789, age 68. As his third wife, he married on 29 March 1791, JOANNA COOKE,

who died on 25 February 1802, age 65. She willed her real estate, a house and land in Cambridge on the Concord Road, to her nephew William Cook of Salem, with smaller bequests to other nephews and nieces, in addition to her step-son Benjamin and his daughter Grace (Middlesex County Probate, First Series, Case no. 11101).

Children (by second marriage) (Wyman, Charlestown Genealogies and Estates, 1:532):
    18. i. Benjamin[5], b. 1 Feb. 1749/50.
    19. ii. Joseph, b.21 Dec.1752.
    20.iii. Isaac, b. 27 July 1756.
        iv. Child, bur. 18 Aug. 1759.

Edward W. Hanson, "The Hurds of Boston," The New England Historical and Genealogical Register, Vol. 132 (April 1978), p. 91.

THE HENRY SYSTEM

    This system of numbering a compiled genealogy derives its name from Reginald Buchanan Henry who used it for his well known Genealogies of the Families of the Presidents (Rutland, Vt.: The Tuttle Co., 1935). Some expert genealogists use this system whereby a series of numbers is used to denote an individual's relationship to the earliest generation

33

discussed. John Frederick Dorman's <u>The
Prestons of Smithfield and Greenfield
in Virginia</u> (Louisville: The Filson
Club, 1982) provides an excellent
example. The system allows you to
determine the number of the father of
that individual and to determine the
order of birth for that individual.
For example, the male in the first
generation discussed is number 1 (one).
His first child becomes number 11 (one-
one; not eleven); his second child
becomes number 12 (one-two), and so on.
Accordingly, the third child of number
11 (one-one) would be numbered 113 (one-
one-three). Any number larger than 9
(any two digit number) is placed in
parentheses, such as 11 (12) (one-one-
twelve), to indicate the twelfth child
of the first child of number 1. While
this system is simple enough and
perfectly "accurate," it does not seem
to have gained favor with a great
number of genealogical writers.

EXAMPLE 3

Elizabeth Preston, eldest child of
William and Susanna (Smith) Preston,
was born 31 May 1762, Augusta Co.,
Va.,[1] and died 4 Feb. 1837, Montgomery
Co., Va.[2] She married 14 Jan. 1779,[3]
"Smithfield," Montgomery Co., Va.,
William Strother Madison, son of John
and Agatha (Strother) Madison,[4] who
died 17 March 1782, near "Madison-

ville," Montgomery Co., Va., aged 29.[5]

William Madison was recommended as a justice of the Botetourt County Court on 14 April 1774 and qualified to that office on 8 Nov. 1774.[6] The faculty of the College of William and Mary gave him the office of the surveyor of Washington County but since it was inconvenient for him to reside there, on 25 March 1777 he entered into an agreement with Robert Preston to perform the duties of that office.[7] He gave bond as sheriff of Botetourt County on 14 Jan. 1780.[8] Later that year he was put in charge of British prisoners captured at King's Mountain.[9] He died of smallpox contracted in military service.[10]

Elizabeth (Preston) Madison resided until her death at "Madison-ville" in Montgomery County. John Madison devised to her a life interest in this land where his son William had lived.[11]

Their children were:[12]
+311 Susanna Smith, married John Howe Peyton.
+312 Agatha Strother, married Garnett Peyton.

John Frederick Dorman, C.G., F.A.S.G., <u>The Prestons of Smithfield and Greenville in Virginia</u>, (Louisville: The Filson Club, 1982), pp. 47-48.

Note: References given at bottom of page.

THE SOSA-STRADONITZ SYSTEM

The Sosa-Stradonitz System is widely used throughout the world by genealogists. It is explained in Pierre Durge's Genealogy: An Introduction to Continental Concepts (New Orleans: Polyanthos, 1977) that the system was invented by 1676 by Jerome de Sosa, a Spanish genealogist, and was revised by Stephane Kekule von Stradonitz in 1898 in his published work. Most genealogists are familiar with the so-called pedigree chart or lineage charts which are widely available from vendors (Refer to Chart).

Most realize that the person whose ancestry is being recorded is No. 1 (one). His father is double that number, or Number 2, and that the mother is that number plus one, or No. 3. Any number can be determined: the father of ancestor No. 20 would be No. 40 and the mother of ancestor No. 20 would be No. 41. (Double 20 and you have the father's number; add one to the father's number and you have found the mother's number). So you can skip unknown ancestors and continue to number. This is an excellent format

when only one line of ancestry is being
traced through several generations or
when you are primarily interested in
compiling the direct ancestry of an
individual in all lines.

EXAMPLE 4

First Generation

1.   Charles II, King of Great Britain,
* St. James's Palace, Westminister 29
May 1630, † Whitehall Palace 6 February
1685, △ Westminister Abbey, 1660 to
Catarina (Catherine), daughter of Joao
IV, King of Portugal, * Villa Vicosa
(Alentejo) 25 November 1638, † Bemposta
Palace, Lisbon, 31 December 1705, △
Santa Maria de Belém. No legitimate
issue.[2]

Second Generation

2.   Charles I, King of Great Britain,
* Dunfermline Palace, Scotland 19
November 1600, † [beheaded] Whitehall
Palace 30 January 1648/9, △ Chapel
Royal, Windsor, 1625, ∞ Paris 1/11 May
1625 [proxy], Canterbury 13/23 June
1625 [in person] to

3.   Henriette Marie, Princess of
France,[3] * Louvre, Paris 26 November
1609, † Colombes (near Paris) 31
August 1669,[4] △ St. Denis.

37

Third Generation

4.   James VI, King of Scotland (James I, King of England), * Edinburgh Castle 19 June 1566, † Theobalds, Herts. 27 March 1625, △ Westminister Abbey, 1567 (Scotland), 1603 (England), ∞ Oslo 23 November 1589 to

5.   Anna, Princess of Denmark, * Skanderborg Castle 12 October 1574, † Hampton Court 2 March 1618/9, △ Westminister Abbey.

6.   Henri IV, King of France and Navarre, * Pau 14 December 1553, † [assassinated] Paris 14 May 1610, △ St. Denis, 1572 (Navarre), 1589 (France), ∞(2) Florence 7 October 1600 [proxy], Lyon 17 December 1600[5] [in person] to

7.   Maria de' Medici, * Florence 26 April 1575,[6] Regent 1610-17, † Cologne 4 July 1642,[7] △ St. Denis.

    Neil D. Thompson, C.G., F.A.S.G. and Col. Charles M. Hansen, U.S.A., "A Medieval Heritage: The Ancestry of Charles II, King of England," The Genealogist, Vol. II, No. 2 (Fall 1981) pp. 161-162.

Note: References for each generation are given after the wife i.e., nos. 6 and 7 (citation after no. 7).

WHICH GENERATION?

Most genealogists use raised Arabic numbers to indicate descent through successive generations. For example, names appear William^6 Smith (John^5, James^4, Andrew^3, Arthur^2, Anthony^1). William Smith is in the sixth generation, the son of John Smith who was in the fifth generation successively from Anthony^1 Smith, the first generation being discussed. This method is not confusing even when raised Arabic numbers are also used for citations. A citation number would never correctly appear in a genealogy where raised Arabic numbers are used between the given and the surname of an individual to denote generation. Nor would a citation number appear after a given name when that given name is used in parentheses after the full name of an individual.

Some genealogists prefer to divide each chapter by generations when using the Register System or the Henry System. Such a designation might appear:

FIRST GENERATION

1.   JOHN^1 SMITH

SECOND GENERATION

3. WILLIAM[2] SMITH (John[1])

A similar procedure can be followed for the Sosa-Stradonitz system for separating generations. Such a format might appear:

FIRST GENERATION

1.

SECOND GENERATION

2.
3.

THIRD GENERATION

4.
5.
6.
7.

A POSTSCRIPT

With the selection of a numbering system, you have selected the format to be used. Be certain that you decide on a numbering system immediately after you state your purpose. Selection of a numbering system at that point in your work will save you many headaches and many hours of extra work. We have learned this lesson by experience, and this is good advice--take it!

Chapter IV

OUTLINING

THE NEED AND USE

Every experienced writer is
convinced of the absolute necessity of
preparing an outline before writing
begins. No builder would ever start a
new building without first having a
blueprint. The blueprint is to a
builder his working plan; the outline
is to the writer his working plan. Few
speakers would ever stand before an
audience without an outline. The
preparation of an outline seems auto-
matic when considering a speech. Yet,
some writers fail to see the importance
of preparing an outline prior to
writing. Just as a specific plan is
vital to the builder and to the
speaker, so it is to the writer. The
absolute need of an outline cannot be
overemphasized.

Consider step-by-step the process
discussed in previous chapters. The
genealogist has drawn from a broad
knowledge and experience, a huge area
of learning--genealogy--supported by a
tremendous number of documents and
research notes. From these raw facts
the potential writer states in general
terms the purpose of the proposed com-

position. The next step is to select a numbering system suited to his purpose, depending upon whether the writer will be dealing with descendants or ancestors. It is now time to organize ideas and select from the research results those facts that will accomplish the writer's purpose in a manner according to acceptable standards.

The outline solves the problem of moving from a seemingly infinite number of documents and raw research notes to an organized composition. The purpose will, to a large extent, determine the plan of organization and presentation.

BASIC RULES

At this point it is important to consider the basic rules in preparing a topic outline. By definition the topic outline will include topics and details expressed in words or phrases--not in complete sentences--in sequence. No verbs are used in topic outlines. Your topic outline will serve as your blueprint for the composition.

TEN POINTS TO REMEMBER ABOUT OUTLINES

1. Uppercase Roman numerals are used for overall topics.
2. Capital letters are used for subtopics

3. Arabic numerals are used for backup points.

4. Periods are used after numerals or letters.

5. Do not use periods after topics or points.

6. Indent two spaces on a typewriter between each numbered or lettered point.

7. Skip one line on a typewriter between each numbered or lettered point.

8. Begin each point with a capital letter.

9. There should be at least two points, but there may be as many as are needed.

10. Use phrases or words, not sentences.

For most genealogists, considerations of overall topics, subtopics, and backup points are usually sufficient. Thus, the form of the outline:

I. First overall topic

    A. Subtopic

        1. Backup point

        2. Backup point

        3. Backup point

    B. Subtopic

        1. Backup point

      2. Backup point

II. Second overall topic

    A. Subtopic

      1. Backup point

      2. Backup point

    B. Subtopic

When a writer is thinking about an overall topic, two important questions should be asked:

1. What is the key to all this information?
2. What am I trying to say?

In considering main topics, the writer should check the key ideas selected against the purpose and make sure the ideas relate to the purpose. Such a consideration will eliminate extraneous or superfluous information. The writer should make sure the details tie the main ideas or topics to the purpose.

ORGANIZING DOCUMENTS AND NOTES

The genealogical writer must have some method of collating raw research notes in order to arrive at a point where facts can be selected. To organize facts chronologically or by date of event is a convenient method of accomplishing this. The writer may arrange facts by strict chronological order without regard to source types. But, in many cases, because of the purpose of the work, the writer may find it is best to arrange all data by source type (*i.e.* census enumerations, land records, wills, *etc.*), and then arrange facts from each type of source in chronological order.

Any consideration and selection of sources to be used involve evaluation on the part of the genealogist. Chronology of facts and chronology of sources do not always coincide. In many cases, the date of the source and the date of the fact will be very different. While all genealogists should seek primary sources (*e.g.*, an eyewitness account of an event), it is not always possible. Too, even primary sources must be evaluated properly. The ability to evaluate sources of every kind, type, form, and description is one test of a good genealogist. The writers of this manual presume that genealogists have a working knowledge of source evaluation. The success of a writer is certainly directly related to his ability as a genealogist.

The ability to select properly evaluated sources, organize the selected sources, and then utilize those sources for a composition often requires patience and practice. While this ability almost seems innate with some, it can be learned. The best way to learn is by doing. The more you write, the easier it becomes, and the better your final compositions become. As you select and organize sources, try to put yourself into the project. Do not allow your work to result in a dull composition that is cold and impersonal. Rather, limited primarily by your purpose, let the work reflect you and be full of life!

No matter which numbering system you select, information about each family is treated as a unit. Content will vary depending upon many factors. However, each unit should probably provide essential vital information so as to identify as completely as possible each named principal in the unit (husbands, wives, and children) by dates and places of birth, marriage, and death. In addition, places of residence, military service, occupations, migrations, and other information may be included. The more information you include, the more interesting your genealogy. Also, pertinent observations and conclusions should be added. Again, the writer's own individual style should be reflected. Do not be afraid to draw conclusions, make observations, or even to ask thought provoking questions. You are the expert who has done the research and has become the most knowledgeable person to write about it.

It is up to the writer to select overall topics and to select material deemed most important and interesting. The final outline will represent the writer's efforts to evaluate, analyze, organize, emphasize the data, and arrange the information in a useful manner. It is much easier to replan and rearrange an outline than it is to rearrange a writer's nearly complete composition. Many consider this one of the major reasons for doing an outline before begining to write. When the writer is satisfied with the plan or outline, actual writing can begin.

DOING YOUR FIRST OUTLINE

There is no better way to learn to outline than by studying the process and then doing one for yourself. You can do it, so do not attempt to write until after the outline is finished.

SAMPLE OUTLINE

I. Father's childhood and youth

   A. Birth

1. Parents, date, place

2. Genetic disorder

B. Status of family

   1. Inheritance from grandfather

   2. Relatives in household

   3. Land and personal property

   4. Influence of religion

   5. Travel with uncle

II. Father as adult

  A. Marriage

    1. Wife's parents, date, place of birth

    2. Influence of her family

  B. Military Service

    1. Militia

    2. Battle participation

  C. Migration

    1. Motives

    2. Search for new home

3. Settlement

D. Death

   1. Date and place

   2. Cause

   3. Funeral and grave location

III. Mother as head of household

A. As planter

   1. Acquisition of new land

   2. Sale or manumission of slaves

B. Death

   1. Date and place

   2. Cause

   3. Funeral and grave location

IV. Children

A. Birth date and place for all

B. Brief information for those not discussed within a separate family unit

   1. Date and place of death

49

2. Date and place of marriage

3. Birth date and place for spouse

4. Date and place of death for spouse

5. Miscellaneous information such as facts of residence, occupation, etc.

Chapter V

WRITING THE TEXT

THE FIRST DRAFT

The time has finally come after all those countless hours of research to commit your results to paper. With your purpose stated, numbering system selected, and your outline as a guide, begin writing. Once you begin writing, set aside an allotted amount of time each day or each week to spend on the project. Begin with your first main topic. Flesh out these people and events, put meat on their bones, and make them come alive, always remembering that all statements must be supported by fact. Using your main topics as a guide, you can probably complete a segment within thirty minutes to an hour of writing time. Do not stop and look up words in the dictionary, *etc*....that can be done later. Allow your thoughts to flow freely through your fingers, into your pen, and onto paper. Do not worry about your style. Style is individual and is a reflection of you, your experiences, your heritage. Your knowledge of the times in which these persons lived may well add flavor to your writing. Do not attempt to imitate another person's style. Do not allow anything to distract you or interrupt your writing time. Use this time for writing--nothing except writing.

The important thing to remember is that you must get something on paper. Try to finish one segment during each writing period. Do not try to think of ideas for future segments. It is very difficult to keep too many ideas in mind at once. CONCENTRATE! Do not quit! If you become bogged down with any part of the first draft, stop and take a brief break. The only way to get your words on paper is to write. At first you may have to use tremendous self-discipline and may even have to force yourself, but stick with this important work. It is the culmination of all your research.

Obviously, there is no way the authors or anyone else can tell you WHAT to write. All anyone can do is suggest the way it should be done. Your article or book is your presentation and interpretation of the facts or information resulting from your research. Write to provide others with (1) an organized summary of your work, (2) facts and opinions, with a clear distinction between each, and (3) connections between seemingly unrelated facts. Let us consider each of these points and think about their importance in your writing.

(1) PROVIDE AN ORGANIZED SUMMARY OF YOUR WORK.

Too many family histories and genealogies fail to do this. Writers do understand that it is their job to organize and summarize their work, but many do not know how to do this. All researchers have seen examples of poorly organized and poorly cited works by genealogists.

EXAMPLE 5 (Poor)

All old DAR papers which were accepted (#'s 3428, 3864, 5769, 6787, *etc.*) and an old family letter said that our John Doe lived in Somerset, Virginia, before the Revolution. Much research done at a great effort and expense proves this is true. The records speak for themselves.

Jones, <u>Early Virginia</u>, page 314:
```
    Doe, J.       -- Somerset Co. 1769
    Doe, John     -- Somerset Co. 1769
    Doe, Jn.      -- Somerset Co. 1769
    Doe, J. B.    -- Somerset Co. 1769
    Doe, John B.-- Somerset Co. 1769
```

Somerset Co., Virginia Wills - By a Professional Researcher:
```
    Doe, Arthur   - 1758
    Doe, Charles  - 1760
    Doe, John     - 1768
    Doe, John B.  - 1773
```

Doe, Wm.   - 1754

Marriages: Somerset County, Virginia
Published Book:

   Book A, page 30--J. Doe to Ann Roe,
30 June 1760
   Same - William Doe to Mayr Roe, 1756
   Ibid.- John Doe to Catherine Roe,
Aug. 18, 1772
   This is ours!

Deed from above:

   Deed A, John Doe and wife Mary on
September 3, 1774 sold land to Richard
(could not read this name which does
not matter) ----"A big oak to a water
course, next to Richard Roe to a pine,
down a creeke to a black jack to the
point of beginning 159 poles"   150
acres   with   all   the   orchards,
........Witnesses: J. B. Doe, James Roe
and signed by his signature mark John
Doe (nice handwriting).

   This is the deed where our ancestor
John Doe sold his land in Somerset
County, Virginia before the American
Revolutionary War. The language of the
old land deed is given as I copied it
so you can see how they followed land.

EXAMPLE 6 (Good)

   A tattered and worn letter dated 5

54

August 1857 written at age eighty-one years by James Doe (No. 38) indicates that his "grandpa had kin folks in Somerset County in the Old Dominion State and had lived there before the War for Independance."[1] Descendants of John Doe have indicated this Virginia residency on lineage papers for the Daughters of the American Revolution.[2] Published and original primary sources document the presence of John Doe in Somerset County, Virginia, prior to 1774.[3] This writer has had no opportunity to conduct sufficient research there to evaluate clues properly from available sources.[4]

Note: All references would be cited fully with appropriate citations to the sources mentioned as clues in Note Four.

(2) PROVIDE MORE FACTS THAN OPINION.

Often genealogists evaluate several facts and draw conclusions. This is what is known as a preponderance of evidence. However, it is important that conclusions made are based on facts that have been determined to be accurate. In this way conclusions become well grounded, and opinions will likely be considered valid.

Richard S. Lackey's article, "A

Previously Unidentified Daughter of Governor Henderson Walker of North Carolina: Genealogical Research and Land Titles," The Genealogist, Vol. 2 (Sept. 1981), pp. 67-73, is a good example of facts and opinion. Documented facts are presented and the article is concluded: "Thus, from evidence of facts which can be proved, the fact of the marriage of Elizabeth Walker to Henry Warren can be inferred." True, there was no record of marriage found and that the marriage ever took place is based entirely on the opinion of the writer as a result of examining the facts which could be found.

Those who read and study this article will readily realize that land titles provide an excellent base upon which to reach sound opinions. Any statement made that is not based on primary evidence in original form is circumstantial. The grounds for the conclusion may be solid or weak. It is up to the writer to provide as many facts as possible based on direct evidence from primary sources searched in original form. In this way, the writer can place opinions on more solid ground.

Most writers realize, for example, that finding two records of a person with the same name does not necessarily constitute a sound base upon which to form a definite conclusion. However, writers tend to fall into this trap unless they exercise caution. Consider the following two examples.

EXAMPLE 7 (Poor)

James Doe found in Eastwood County, Georgia, at the time of the federal census in 1820 is living in Gulf County, Alabama, in 1830, when the federal census was taken there.

Note: That the James Doe found on the 1820 Census of Eastwood County, Georgia, is the identical James Doe found on the 1830 Census of Gulf County, Alabama, is an opinion or conclusion that is very weak. The only FACT presented is that two men named James Doe appear on an 1820 and an 1830 Census of two Southern States.

EXAMPLE 8 (Good)

James Doe, age thirty to forty, along with a wife in the same age bracket, resided with twenty-two slaves in Eastwood County, Georgia, in 1820, and was enumerated next to Zachariah Mucklefuss IV on the census there. The 1830 Census of Gulf County, Alabama, shows a James Doe, age forty to fifty years with no wife and one male child under five years, living there with twenty-eight slaves and listed two lines away from Zachariah Mucklefuss IV. Chronology, slave ownership, and association with the neighbor Zachariah Mucklefuss IV appear to indicate that both enumerations refer to the identical man.

Note: In both examples, the same two census records are used and James Doe appeared on the two census enumerations of the two Southern States given in the first example and is also found on the second. Four other facts are presented. First, the fact of the age and family composition; second, the fact of a large slave ownership; third, the fact of the possible association with Mucklefuss; fourth, the uniqueness of the name, Zachariah Mucklefuss IV. These four facts provide much stronger ground for the opinion by the writer that the two records are records of the identical James Doe.

It is always important to distinguish between fact and opinion. In the second example above, there is no question that the records indicate the facts reported. However, notice that the final statement in example two is clearly an opinion that to this writer "...(facts) appear to indicate..." Whereas, in the first example above, the writer's opinion that the two records for James Doe were for the identical man is not clearly distinguished from the fact.

(3) PROVIDE CONNECTIONS AMONG SEEMINGLY UNCONNECTED FACTS.

After countless hours of working with documents and research notes, genealogists gain a certain "feeling" about records. How many times have you thought to youself, "I KNOW this is right, but I do not have any proof of how I know it." Often genealogists do not stop to ask themselves an important question. That is, "What is the connecting link among all these facts?" The answer will be different for every research situation, but it is up to the writer to identify that connecting link and point it out to the readers.

Think carefully about your own work. That connecting link is possibly a tract of land, the presence of unusual items repeated on estate inventories and in wills, or repeated similarity of names or associates. Once you consciously begin to identify links, then it will be easier to provide your reader with connections among seemingly unconnected facts.

BE DIRECT

Writing should be direct. You should write as an authority on the

59

subject. Be specific as to your
meaning. Think about the fact(s) you
wish to communicate to your reader, and
state specific facts so that others can
reasonably evaluate your work and your
conclusions as they are presented.

EXAMPLE 9 (Poor)

John Richard Doe was the son of
Thomas and Mary Doe. Many genealogists
claim she was the daughter of John Roe,
because of land and will records, most
agree she was the daughter of Richard
Smith. This writer agrees since her
child was referred to in the Will of
Richard Smith.

Note: It is difficult to know the
specific meaning the writer is
attempting to convey in this example.

EXAMPLE 10 (Good)

John Richard Doe was the son of
Thomas Doe and his wife Mary, whose
maiden name has not been conclusively
proved. There is published disagree-
ment as to her maiden name. Because of
a deed from John Roe to Thomas Doe
which acknowledges receipt of what one
writer has called '"a rather minor
consideration" and because the will of
John Roe names a daughter Mary without
any surname given, many genealogists

accept the opinion that Mary, wife of Thomas Doe, was the daughter of John Roe. However, most genealogists, including this writer, accept that Mary was probably the daughter of Richard Smith. It can be proved conclusively that a Richard Smith married a sister of Mary, the wife of Thomas Doe. Further, the will of Richard Smith, dated 3 August 1851, names "my kinsman John Richard Doe, son of the sister of my wife." Indeed, other research is needed to prove that testator Richard Smith is the identical Richard Smith who married the sister of Mary, wife of Thomas Doe.

Note: The facts and conclusions are stated more clearly by the writer in example 10.

USE PERTINENT INFORMATION

Be careful to select details that are pertinent and that add clarity to writing. Do not fill your article or book with details that are of no significance to your purpose. The authors recall reading the following information in a colonial Maryland genealogy:

"The family owned the tract called "Arthur's Adventure." In 1905, a tract by a similar name, "Arthur's Choice," was donated to the county for a park. The park fell into disrepair, and today it is a used car lot specializing in truck sales."

BE HONEST AND OPEN

Writers should use extracts and direct quotes from records to add clarity and support their own writing. Quoted passages from original documents add flavor and help capture the time period under consideration. However, be careful that you do not take a quote out of context in order to support a point you wish to make.

EXAMPLE 11

If the actual document states: "My trusted, loyal and loving brother in the church, James Doe," do NOT quote the document as stating: "My trusted, loyal and loving brother, James Doe."

Most genealogists today would find it inconceivable to think that a writer would do such a thing, but it does happen. Be honest with all writing, and never conceal research results which produce conflicting information. Rather, point out any and all such conflicts. Remember that genealogists consider ALL available information. Also, take great care in suggesting that one record is "incorrect" when it does not agree with others. After all, just because a record is different does not necessarily make it wrong. Certainly, some records are indeed wrong, but extreme care should be taken in drawing such a conclusion.

EXAMPLE 12

John Doe was born 10 July 1840.[1] ...(Part of paragraph omitted)... As a young man, he sold real property on 29 August 1856.[9]

----

[1]Headstone inscription for John Doe, Smith Cemetery, Oak Co., Ala. (NW^4 SW^4, S14, T4N-R13E, Kingville P.M.). Author's visit 15 Aug. 1975. 1880 U.S. Census (Population Schedule), Oak Co., Ala., p. 400, Family 389, Dwelling 381, Lines 16-19, (N.A. Mf. M-805, roll 15). This and other census records are in error as to his birth.

[9]"Deed of Sale from John Doe to Richard Smith" (Recorded 30 Sept. 1858) Oak Co., Ala., Deed Bk. A, pp. 302-325, Office of the Probate Judge, Oakville, Ala. Photocopy of original in possession of author.

EXAMPLE 13

Records conflict as to the exact

birth year of John Doe. His tombstone inscription indicates 10 July 1840,[1] and other records conflict.[2] He was most likely born ca. 1835.[3]

---

[1] Cite headstone as above.

[2] Cite census as above showing age 42

[3] Cite deed above. He had to be over twenty-one years of age in 1856 to sell real property in his own capacity. This is the most convincing proof that he was not born in 1840. The John Doe who sold land in August 1856 obviously was twenty-one years of age. The tombstone giving his birthdate as 10 July 1840 is apparently wrong for three reasons: (1) the decedent did not give the stonemason his year of birth, (2) the person who gave his birth year may not have known it, and (3) the tombstone may have been erected years later when all who would have remembered his birth were dead.

Do not attempt to conceal weak points in research. If you have not had an opportunity or have not taken time to examine a record that you know perfectly well should be checked, then say so. Attempts at concealing lack of research or weak points in research will be detected by a knowledgeable reader.

EXAMPLE 14 (Poor)

The 1860 population census schedule for River County, Alabama, disclosed a personal property value of $30,000.00 for John Doe. Doe probably owned as many as thirty or forty slaves and was a planter at the time.

EXAMPLE 15 (Good)

The 1860 population census schedule for River County, Alabama, disclosed a personal property value of $30,000.00 for John Doe. It is probable that this value reflects slave property, but the 1860 slave schedule was not examined.

DRAW CONCLUSIONS

Conclusions can be provocative. Excellent research and analysis of your work may raise more questions than provide answers. Do not be afraid to ask questions that are raised as a result of your research. Again, you know your subjects best. If questions are raised in your own mind about a point, it is usually a good idea to pose these questions to your readers.

One of your authors in an article on Thomas Berry (Donald Ray Barnes,

"Berry-Baccus-Peach-Stephens: Some Northern Neck of Virginia Family Relationships". <u>The Virginia Genealogist</u>, Vol. 26 (Jan.-Mar. 1982), pp. 8-10) wrote of him:

"His signature on all documents is very legible, which is odd! Here we have a man, bred for no trade, a man who had been a sailor and in his later years a shoemaker, making the poorest of shoes, with a remarkably good signature. Why? If Thomas Berry knew how to read and write as his signature implies, then why so little success in his lifetime? Was he a younger son of a good family whom success eluded, or did he elude success?"

BE SERIOUS

Do not attempt to be overly witty or amusing with your writing. Reader use and enjoyment does not depend on these factors. The authors could cite many examples where such attempts ruin otherwise good genealogical work. Most people gain tremendous pleasure and enjoyment from doing genealogical research. Some never consider this pleasurable activity as being scholarly. But, genealogy is a scholarly endeavor. Take it seriously, and let your writing reflect this attitude. We hope the following illustrates the point being made:

EXAMPLE 16 (Poor)

One writer, in reporting that an ancestor owned a "large copper still" at the time of his death, added: "probably to cool???? his milk in!!!!" (*sic.*)

This is not to say that amusing events or accounts should not be included. Indeed they should. Certainly, true life can be funny. One of your authors recently included the following in a published genealogy:

"Once when the family was entertaining very distinguished guests, lunch had been prepared one summer day and placed on a table in an open hallway. The dogs chased a large goat into the yard, and the goat ran and jumped into the middle of the table of food as the family and guests ate."

This account is still recalled by the family, and it gives real meaning to the admonition used in this family when preparing a meal for important guests, "Watch out for the goat!"

TRAPS FOR WRITERS

All multiple marriages should be clearly noted in any family history or genealogy. Those having children by more than one spouse will need to be documented separately. It continues to amaze your authors to find so many genealogies with their own Biblical Sarah. Few women past their mid-forties give birth to children. When genealogists find such possible births, it is a definite clue that there may be more than one wife involved. When a man had two or more wives (perhaps with the same given name), the genealogist has problems, especially in the absence of good marriage records. Always try to list children with the parent to whom they belong.

EXAMPLE 17

Issue of John Doe and wife Mary Roe

+2.	i.	John Doe
+3.	ii.	Mary Doe
+4.	iii.	Richard Doe
+5.	iv.	Jane Doe

Issue of John Doe and wife Mary (?)

+6.	v.	James Doe
+7.	vi.	Donald Doe
+8.	vii.	June Doe

Genealogical writers should use extreme caution in the linkage between generations. The same care should be taken as if you were completing a lineage paper for one of the hereditary societies. Make as strong and as positive an identification as is possible when connecting generations in a compiled genealogy. Many researchers find a will, perhaps for a William Brown, in Virginia. They cite the will as proof that he had a son, James Brown. The next thing you know, you have picked up a James Brown in North Carolina or Georgia twenty years later. These writers offer no proof that the James Brown of North Carolina or Georgia is the identical James, son of William Brown, who was the Virginia testator. To make matters worse, they may even provide information that will indicate to the reader that they were probably NOT the identical man. Unless you have proof of a connecting link between generations, it would be best to write that "the parents are unknown." Mention should be made of research conducted to attempt to prove parentage, the results of that search, and possible conclusions. Also, note in the remarks on citations that the authors of this book emphasize that all statements linking one generation to another MUST BE FULLY CITED.

HISTORICAL EVENTS AND PERSPECTIVE

Knowing major historical events is a must for a good genealogical writer.

The War Between the States and the resulting political events in the South made Texas very attractive. The Gold Rush served as an inducement for migration to California, and Utah offered New Zion to the Mormons. Mentioning--correctly mentioning--historical events gives you an additional base needed to put meat onto those ancestral bones. All of a sudden you can hear the conestoga wagons roll across the plains; Brigham Young declaring, "This is the place!"; the railroad spikes being driven into the crossties from one end of America to the other. Your ancestors will cease to be names and dates. They will be lifted off the pages of forgotten history and assume their place in our heritage, standing beside all those who have gone before us and those who will come after us, for time and eternity.

Genealogists attempting to write should be able to evaluate the activities, circumstances, records, and lives of ancestors in historical perspective. Maybe our ancestors did not have exactly the same values or sense of justice that we have today. But, would we have our same values and sense of justice had we lived in their circumstances at the same time and place? Writers should not judge ancestors on the basis of society today. If you are writing about the eighteenth century on the Southern frontier, then you need to have some grasp of the values and the feeling of the place and time. Too often writers view their ancestors only in the context of the present and fail to place ancestors--or, for that matter, the records of those ancestors--in proper historical perspective.

USE ILLUSTRATIONS AND CHARTS

Use exhibits such as maps, charts, documents, and pictures. The value of visual aids is well known. Photographs of ancestors, their property, or their possessions assist us in putting them into proper perspective. The ancestors come alive. They walk! They breathe! Living descendants often can see physical likenesses to themselves upon seeing a picture or photograph of early ancestors. Every descendant cannot own ancestral furniture, silver, earthen pots, or other memorabilia, but most descendants would appreciate a photo-graph of such items. Make good use of maps to indicate where your ancestors lived. Use charts to show relation-ships. Also, reproduction of original records can make a publication more interesting and valuable.

You are now ready to type your first draft---mistakes and all. How proud you will be of your work! It is yours--your thoughts, the result and

culmination of hours of research and
work. Re-read the first draft, correct
the spelling and grammatical errors,
insert new thoughts in the margins, and
now you should take a most difficult
step. You must serve as the most
critical judge of your work by asking
yourself if you have accomplished your
goals. Do the people, places, and
times come to life? Is the writing
clear, concise, and logical? Can the
reader distinguish clearly between
presentation of facts and opinions?
Are all the facts presented? Give a
copy--always keep the original in your
possession--to another person who will
read it objectively and make suggestions. Another person will be able to
determine if you have said what you are
trying to say and if you have made the
points you want to make.

Chapter VI

THE FINAL DRAFT

THE FINISHING TOUCH

Effective communication with the reader should be the objective of all writers. Specifically, genealogical writers must strive to communicate research results to readers. The best way to communicate is to write clearly and succinctly. This can be difficult. Be sure that the words you select convey the intended meaning and that all pronouns are clearly understood. These seem to be two major problems for genealogists.

Your article or book should always be written using proper English. All words should be correctly spelled, using no contractions and only standard abbreviations. A reader will immediately notice misspelled words or incorrect grammar. The first impression is often what will determine the review or the evaluation your work will receive. Misspelled words, misused words, or the wrong tense are all too obvious. A cardinal rule (NO EXCEPTIONS): Have your manuscript proofread.

Writing styles have changed over

the years. There was a time when "I" and "we" would not appear in this type of publication. However, your authors feel that the use of the third person is still generally the best course to follow for a compiled genealogy. Remember:

1st person (The person speaking.): "I think the record is accurate."

2nd person (The person spoken to.): "You will find the record accurate."

3rd person (The person or thing spoken about.): "The record will be found to be accurate," or "He will find the record accurate."

Your original attempt at writing your family history or genealogy should be done with such care and consideration that the final revision or final draft really is not too much more than proofreading. If you find that you are making drastic changes in your final revision, then you probably are not being careful enough with your first attempts or original efforts.

Prior to publication, writers should consider submitting their work to a professional genealogist for final editing. In addition to both the authors, many other Certified Genealogists listed on the current list available from the Board For Certification of Genealogists, Post Office Box 19165, Washington, D. C. 20036, offer a consultation service to edit manuscripts for a fee. Generally, such work is done by the job, so you will know the fee before professional editing by a genealogist begins. Many writers could have prevented embarrassing reviews if only they had had their work edited by a knowledgeable professional genealogist prior to publication. Some genealogical publishers offer this as a service to their authors.

An unsigned article, "Writing and Publishing Genealogical Book Reviews," Association of Professional Genealogists Newsletter, Vol. 2 (May-June 1980), p. 2, not copyrighted, published by Roger Scanland, editor, says: "A family history which merits a review is one so poorly done as to call for a cautionary review, or one so well done that it:

1. Is well documented, mainly from primary (original) sources.

2. Seeks to place the family in its historical, social, and geographic context.

3. Is interesting to read without being maudlin or sensational.

4. Avoids speculation ("So-and-so is

believed to have been born in...")
unless the author marshalls some good
reasons for such statements.

5. Avoids perpetuating legendary
statements (ancestors who were suppos-
edly generals, bodyguards to a well-
known person, cheated out of property
in the Old Country, etc.) unless such
statements are clearly identified as
unproved.

6. Does not launder its sources by
correcting spelling and grammar errors
in quoted material. Normally, source
materials should be altered only when
confusion would result or when greater
conciseness is necessary.

7. Avoids manipulation of data to
gloss over research problems
encountered by the author.

8. Is reasonably free from errors in
grammar, syntax, and typography.

9. Is indexed at least by surname and
personal name, and preferably by
selected topics as well.

10. Does not duplicate a work already
in print unless the earlier work is
inferior or is outdated."

Chapter VII

PROBLEMS AND ADVICE

At each workshop your authors have
conducted about writing a family
history or genealogy, problems on
certain subjects seem to surface. In
the past, we have often referred
querists to Noel C. Stevenson's The
Genealogical Reader (New Orleans:
Polyanthos, 1977), especially to the
following articles: "Tradition and
Family History," "Royal Ancestry," and
"Fraudulent Pedigrees," by Donald Lines
Jacobus; "Pitfalls in Genealogical
Research," by Milton Rubincam; "English
and American Heraldry" and "English
Feudal Genealogy," by G. Andrews
Moriarty. These writers have discussed
in the articles mentioned above many of
the points of interest to genealogical
writers. We feel the readers of this
manual may also want suggested current
recommendations on certain "popular"
subjects: (1) Selection of a Title, (2)
Coats of Arms, (3) Adoptions, (4)
Skeletons, (5) Medical Information, (6)
Conflicting Information, and (7)
Inferred Relationships.

SELECTING A TITLE

It is most important to select the
best possible title for your article or
book. We feel that a title should have

the elements of name, date, and place. For example, John and Mary (Smith) Jones of York County, Maine, and Rowan County, North Carolina, 1680-1800. A title like the above quickly tells a user if he wishes to look at this work. It also tells you that the work concerns the family of John and Mary (Smith) Jones who lived in York County, Maine, and in Rowan County, North Carolina, in the period 1680-1800. Your title is the first impression the potential reader will have of your article or book. It should not only be descriptive, but it should also create interest and need.

A writer may wish to use a short title and add in the sub-title the elements of name, date, and place. For example, A Jones Family History may be the title, but the subtitle might be John and Mary (Smith) Jones of York County, Maine, and Rowan County, North Carolina, 1680-1800. The final determination of the title of your publication is your decision.

Be honest with your title. If your selected title is The King Family, you would reasonably be expected to have covered all members of the King family, at least in America. A King Genealogy might be more discriptive and honest. Think about your title. If yours is a work covering Some Descendants of John King, son of

78

<u>Randolph</u> <u>King</u> <u>of</u> <u>Any</u> <u>County</u>, <u>New</u> <u>York</u>,
<u>1690-1776</u>, consider using the subtitle
if you <u>do</u> not like using a long title.
For example, <u>A</u> <u>King</u> <u>Genealogy</u>: <u>Some</u>
<u>Descendants</u> <u>of</u> <u>John</u> <u>King</u>, <u>son</u> <u>of</u>
<u>Randolph</u> <u>King</u> <u>of</u> <u>Any</u> <u>County</u>, <u>New</u> <u>York</u>,
<u>1690-1776</u>.

ADVICE: A title should be descriptive
and should include name, date, and
place.

<u>COATS</u> <u>OF</u> <u>ARMS</u>

It seems all genealogies must have
a reproduction of a coat of arms. We
know all the arguments! Many otherwise
well researched, well documented, and
well cited genealogies are clouded with
inclusion of a coat of arms just for
the sake of having one. It is
sufficient to carry your research to
the immigrant, make possible suggestions for additional research, and
mention that one or one hundred
families of a particular surname bore
arms. But, please, do not include this
for inclusion's sake. It stains all
those hours of credible research.

If you feel you absolutely must
include a coat of arms in order to
satisfy the family, be certain to
explain that the selected coat of arms
probably has no significance at all to
anyone named in the book.

ADVICE: Unless you have a proved armorial line, do not include a coat of arms.

ADOPTEES

The writers of this publication are fully aware of the fact that a child's parents are the persons who rear it, feed it, rock it to sleep, tend to cuts and bruises, and are there to listen in time of need. As genealogists we are also aware that we trace our genetic ancestry. If we have an ancestor who was adopted and have no clue to his family origin or surname, then in each succeeding generation our number of unidentified ancestors doubles.

It is perfectly satisfactory to trace the ancestry of adoptive parents as well as natural parents. In this situation or any other situation that involves adoptees, we need to cite accurately and truthfully.

EXAMPLE 18

Issue of James Jones and June Smith, his wife:

    i. (Adopted) John Jones[1]
   ii. Mary Jones

[1]Any Co., Mich., Adoption file no. 614, Court Records 1902-1914. Copy in possession of author.

ADVICE: Always indicate a known or suspected adoption in a genealogy.

FAMILY SKELETONS

Many later lineal or collateral descendants may be squeamish about a family containing prisoners, murders, divorces, illegitimacy, *etc.* Some writers will, no doubt, consider certain social, ethnic, or religious differences as skeletons. Every family has skeletons! Obviously, some of these facts may need to be mentioned to maintain a genetic ancestry. Possibly you may not wish to say that great-grandmother and great-grandfather did not bother to get married. If you know some fact or can document some fact which you do not wish to publish, then cite the locale of the information and instruct serious researchers to look at this record. Always cite facts accurately and truthfully. This material is being published to aid future researchers. Sometimes the human qualities of our ancestors make them come alive. The reason some of your ancestors failed to marry may add pages of material to your manuscript and will often furnish additional clues for further research.

Obviously, any question of illegitimacy in one's lineage is a touchy subject, but concealing it is not the solution. You do future generations a great injustice by not telling the truth, for those who follow will be researching wrong lines. Errors of ancestry double each generation. There can be many reasons that the parents of the child never married. Sometimes our most interesting ancestral lines are those without benefit of clergy. However, one should take great care in claiming to be an illegitimate member of a family.

ADVICE: Be truthful without inflicting pain.

MEDICAL INFORMATION

With the increased interest and emphasis on genetic studies, many genealogists attempt to document certain traits or diseases. Why are you a blue-eyed, freckled-faced, redhead with a brown-eyed, swarthy skinned brother or sister with straight coal black hair? Does the presence of hemophilia, sickle cell anemia, high blood pressure, cancer, or heart disease have any importance to a genealogist? Consanguinity, marriage between close relatives, should be included in any medical information.

Such marriages reduce the gene-pool for descendants. Historically the Church, and later the State, had to give approval for a marriage, and there are many references in early Church records which interest genealogists.

A learned geneticist has said that we should attempt to trace all descendants from our great-great-grandparents and document physical appearance, traits, medical history, and cause of death for each. Any medical information must, of course, include insanity, alcoholism, drug addiction, and various diseases--all of which may effect genetic inheritance. In addition, superior intellect, longevity, absence of illness, and any other desirable characteristic should also be noted. Genetics is a research field in its infancy. Who can envision what the work of future genealogists or the work we are doing today can contribute to our health and to those who follow us?

ADVICE: Include major medical information or citations in any complete family history or genealogy so that the facts can be determined.

CONFLICTING INFORMATION

Every genealogist is, from time to time, confronted with the discovery of conflicting information. A genealogist weighs all the evidence before rendering a judgment, conclusion, or opinion on a fact or a source. We suggest readers obtain a copy of Noel C. Stevenson's Genealogical Evidence (Laguna Hills, CA: Aegean Park Press, 1979). It is important to state why you used or selected particular evidence. What convinced you of its greater weight or worth?

ADVICE: Always cite any evidence which is found that is contrary to other evidence.

INFERRED RELATIONSHIPS

If the need to include coats of arms in not enough, then the complusive urge to "appropriate ancestry" seems overwhelming to some writers. Many genealogies begin with two or three generations of a family living in the fourteenth century, and then leapfrog to a seventeenth century ancestor living in America. To make matters worse, the point of origin of the American ancestor cannot be determined. It is natural to want to be descended from families of noble or gentry status, and many are. Prove each generation starting with yourself, weighing and evaluating all the evidence. You do not leap from Richard Smith living in Boone County, Ohio, in

1810 to John Smith living in York County, Maine, in 1680 to Adam Smith living in Chesterfield, Derbyshire, England, in 1585. Even if Adam had a son John who went to New England--MORE PROOF IS NEEDED.

ADVICE: Be sure that inferred relationships are clearly distinguished from proved relationships.

Chapter VIII

CITATIONS AND BIBLIOGRAPHY

Write It Right is a companion
volume to Cite Your Sources. All
genealogists should have a copy of each
to use as reference tools when documenting and writing family histories or
genealogies. This chapter uses some
basic facts found in Cite Your Sources.

THE NOTE ENTRY:

Details regarding components in a
note entry for (1) Books, Pamphlets and
Monographs; (2) Serials; and (3)
Unpublished Documents will follow
later. In addition, short or second
use of notes will be discussed. Every
entry in all notes contains certain
elements, and first citations differ
depending upon the type of source and
the factors regarding that source.
Certain elements are common to all
citations:

PUNCTUATION. The necessary items of
basic information are presented as a
note by the researcher in proper
sequence and with certain punctuation
marks. The insertion of punctuation
marks in and between elements of a
simple book citation is illustrated in

the following example:

[1]F. Wilbur Helmbold, _Tracing Your Ancestry_ (Birmingham: Oxmoor House, 1976), p. 8.

More complicated notes may require some additional punctuation. The researcher may generally be guided by standard rules concerning the use of punctuation marks within the body of an entry. Punctuation should be used as a device to clarify meaning.

CAPITALIZATION. Basic rules of English grammar should be followed for capitalization.

ABBREVIATION. Abbreviations should be utilized to save space. Researchers are familiar with the common abbreviations of months and states; these should be used in notes for economy of space. Always be consistent with abbreviations. For example, use standard state abbreviations (Tenn., Miss., Wash.) all the time, or use those used by the United States Postal Service (TN, MS, WA), but never use a combination of the two (TN, Miss., WA). Again, be consistent.

In addition, other widely accepted abbreviations can be used. Always keep in mind that clarity is more important than saving space. Any abbreviation can be devised by a writer for specific sources for which frequent references are made. These would be used in second and later references to that source. This is advisable because it will conserve space and will save time. But, the citation to that source MUST be given in full the first time that source is used, and it should be followed with a note calling attention to the abbreviation used thereafter.

EXAMPLE 19

First citation to a source that will be used frequently thereafter:

[1]Records of the Court of Pleas and Quarter Sessions (hereinafter cited RCPQS), Bertie Co., N.C. (hereinafter cited Bertie), Bk. II, p. 402, Courthouse, Windsor, N.C. (unless cited to the contrary, it shall be understood that all citations to Bertie shall be located there), Copy in possession of author (hereinafter, "Author" shall mean copies in author's possession).

Later citations can make use of the abbreviations and word citations explained in note number one.

[2]"Deed of Gift from John Smith to John Doe," 3 March 1755 (recorded 10 June 1755), Deed Bk. 13, pp. 402-405, Bertie, Author.

[3] RCPQS, Bk. III, p. 100, Bertie, Author.

THE USE OF REFERENCE NOTES:

While the primary purpose of reference notes is to provide authority and credibility to the information presented, the researcher should consider the overall use of notes. A variety of notes can be used to make genealogical work meaningful. The genealogist should have a clear understanding of the use of notes so as to achieve desired results. The basic uses follow:

1. To cite the exact source of information.

2. To make cross references to information.

3. To explain, add information, and make statements which amplify the text or cited source.

4. To make acknowledgements.

Writers should take special note of the fact that certain points in a family history or compiled genealogy MUST have a reference note. For example, always cite any direct quote; always cite any statement that proves a link in a relationship; and always give the citation for any point of controversy. Your authors also think that an amplification of the text is in order any time words of restriction are used such as "it appears" or "it is probably" as an explanation of the doubt to aid other researchers. Never fail to acknowledge the assistance of others--thank them for their help.

BOOKS, PAMPHLETS, AND MONOGRAPHS

THE ENTRY. Citations for all books, pamphlets, and other monographic publications are designed to identify the reference. A complete first reference entry for a book should always include four simple basic information items: A. the author entry, B. the complete title, C. publication facts, and D. page number(s). Proper sequence or order of presenting this information is always maintained even if some items are unnecessary or do not apply. With the exception of the page number(s), the title page (front and back) of most books usually provides the information required.

EXAMPLE 20

[1]Natalie Maree Belting, Kaskaskia Under the French Regime (New Orleans: Polyanthos, 1975), p. 82.

SERIALS

Serials may be defined as publications issued in successive parts at
intervals. Note should be made that a
serial differs from a multi-volume work
and a named series. Many libraries
will bind issues of a complete volume
of a serial which may resemble a volume
in a named series or a multi-volume
work, and care must be taken to observe
the difference. Two major types of
serials are A. Periodicals and B.
Newspapers.

A. PERIODICALS. The publication plan
for most genealogical periodicals is
quarterly. Each issue is usually
identified by month issued (such as
January, April, July, October) or by
the season (Spring, Summer, Fall,
Winter). Each issue is usually
numbered, and a stated number of issues
constitutes a volume. Many genealogical periodicals publish articles or
record abstracts in installments that
may run for several issues or volumes.
The first complete reference for notes
for an item from a periodical should
include the following basic information
given in the following order: 1. name
of author(s), 2. title of the article,
3. name of the periodical, 4. volume of
the periodical, 5. month/season of year
issued, and 6. page number(s).

EXAMPLE 21

[1]Lawrence K. Wells, "William Henry of Henry's Knob," The South Carolina Magazine of Ancestral Research, IV (Winter 1976), p. 24.

B. NEWSPAPERS. A first reference to a newspaper will probably differ slightly from a standard note for other periodicals. The following elements should be used by genealogists when citing a reference from a newspaper: 1. name of the newspaper (place of publication), 2. date of the issue, 3. page numbers as well as section and column numbers if considered necessary, and 4. location (where newspapers are found).

EXAMPLE 22

[1]Disseminator (Brandon, Rankin Co., Miss.) 21 Feb. 1844, p. 2; Miss. Dept. of Archives and History, Jackson.

UNPUBLISHED DOCUMENTS

The majority of sources cited by genealogists will ideally consist of references to original unpublished documents and manuscripts. Because of the great variety of such sources utilized by modern genealogists, it seems impractical to attempt to consider anything other than a suitable broad standard form. In all cases, it will be necessary for the genealogist to use good judgment in citing original documents. Because of the frequent use of some documents by genealogists, detailed considerations are given to many specific catagories in Cite Your Sources.

BASIC FORM FOR MISCELLANEOUS UNPUBLISHED DOCUMENTS. Most unpublished documents can be cited according to this basic suggested form. The following items of information should be included in the following order: 1. descriptive title of the document, 2. significant dates or numbers, 3. specific location of the document used, and 4. form used and/or repository.

EXAMPLE 23

[1]Prince George's County, Maryland Court Proceedings 1720-1722, Liber K, p. 488, Hall of Records, Annapolis.

SHORT OR SECOND USE OF NOTES

As observed, the first time a reference note appears it must always be presented in complete form. However, when a second or subsequent reference is made to a note which has been cited in full form, a short citation may be employed. Never use a short form as a first reference to a work. The circumstances will determine the proper shortened form.

A. SHORT TITLE REFERENCE. A reference to a work previously fully cited, but not immediately following the citation in full form, should use the short title form. Information should include the following: 1. the last name or surname only of the author, 2. a short form of the title, and 3. the page number(s).

EXAMPLE 24

[1]Helmbold, <u>Ancestry</u>, p. 168.

B. OTHER SHORT REFERENCE FORMS. When a reference to a work previously fully cited follows immediately, another short reference form can be used. The Latin abbreviation <u>Ibid</u>. may be used to save space. Note that this short reference must be to the complete citation immediately preceding and cannot be used to refer to a preceding work when there is an intervening reference.

EXAMPLE 25

[1]Richard S. Lackey, C.G.,

F.A.S.G., Cite Your Sources (New Orleans: Polyanthos, Inc., 1980), p. 20.

[2]Ibid., p. 21.

Once reference notes have been written, it becomes necessary to decide on the location of those notes. They can be (1) placed at the foot of each page as "footnotes," (2) placed at the end of each chapter of a book or at the end of an article as "endnotes," or (3) placed in parentheses or brackets in the text. There is no single correct way, but your writers recommend the use of endnotes. Many researchers have probably noticed that some editors, such as George Ely Russell, C.G., F.A.S.G., editor of the National Genealogical Society Quarterly, place "Notes and References" at the end of articles.

Reference or citation numbers for notes should follow the information to which they refer. Place an Arabic numeral slightly above (raised)--about half way above--the line. Do not use a period, slash, parenthesis, or bracket with a reference number. Raised Arabic note numbers should be consecutive and run continuously throughout an article or chapter of a book.

If actual citation notes are placed

at the bottom or foot of each page, the reference numbers on that page must have the notes for those references located on the same page.

Many writers place reference notes in the text or make abbreviated or short citations to a longer citation in a selected bibliography. This is not recommended for a compiled genealogy. Problems arise when a writer tries to make use of a note to amplify the text or to provide a content note. This method of placing notes in the text is great for some types of writing--not for genealogy. For example, the writers have used it for this manual. However, for most family histories and genealogies it proves most unsatisfactory.

BIBLIOGRAPHY

A bibilography is a compilation of sources on a particular subject. If it is not restricted, a bibliography should include every available source used on a subject. It is rare, however, that a writer can include every source available on a subject. The terms "Sources Consulted" or "Selected Bibliography" are usually a more accurate description of the writer's work. Except when a bibliography or appropriate heading is very short, sections are used to divide the sources. Most genealogical writers find it convenient to divide a bibliography according to source types such as (1) Primary Sources and (2) Secondary Sources. Under each heading one might further subdivide. Many writers commonly subdivide by location of the sources: The National Archives, Washington, D. C.; The Hall of Records, Annapolis, Maryland; or Any City Public Library, Any City, Any State.

Within each division and each subdivision, arrangement of entries should have a definite order. Many writers arrange sources alphabetically by first letter of author's surname for published materials and by chronological order for unpublished materials. Any plan of arrangement that would not be obvious to the reader should be explained at the beginning.

Any bibliography may be annotated by the writer. Annotations may explain or amplify the use of the source. If annotations are used extensively, the writer may consider using a heading such as "Annotated Selected Bibliography."

Essentially the same information is given in a bibliographical entry that is presented in a full note entry, but in a different sequence.

EXAMPLE 26

For a Note Entry:

[1]Ellen Gillespie, <u>Descendants</u> <u>of</u>
<u>Robert</u> <u>Gillespie</u> <u>(1800-1862)</u> <u>of</u>
<u>Virginia</u> (Richmond: Globe Publishers,
1902), p. 10.

For a Bibliographical Entry:

Gillespie, Ellen, <u>Descendants</u> <u>of</u>
   <u>Robert</u> <u>Gillespie</u> <u>(1800-1862)</u>
   <u>of</u> <u>Virginia</u>. Richmond: Globe
   Publishers, 1902.

Most genealogical writers who use
complete and extensive footnotes will
find a bibliography unnecessary.
However, writers who wish to use short
citations in the text will need--rather
must have--a full bibliography.

EXAMPLE 27

TEXT: "Robert Gillespie removed in
1820 to Any County, Virginia.
(Gillespie, <u>Descendants</u>, p. 104.) He
took his family to..."

Note: A reader would expect and would
have to have an extensive bibliography
to make any use of such a citation.

Chapter IX

MECHANICS

As the writer you are responsible
for the entire article or book. We
have never seen a review which read,
"the writer did an excellent job, but
the typist, or printer was careless."
Most editors and printers want writers
to examine and correct the final copy
prior to publication. A printer,
unlike an editor, will not make any
suggestions for improvement. Most
editors simply return undesirable work
rather than going to the trouble of
making improvement suggestions. It is
up to the writer to see to it that a
clear, correct, typed, original copy of
the manuscript is submitted to an
editor or printer. This is true
whether you as writer double as typist
or whether you hire a typist. The
writer is responsible!

<u>SUGGESTIONS</u>

1. Use 8 1/2" x 11" good quality
typing paper.

2. Use pica type.

3. Use a good quality carbon ribbon.

4. Use at least one inch (1") margins

on all four sides of the paper. On the first page of every major division, leave a top two inch (2") margin.

5.   Indent paragraphs five (5) spaces for the first word of the first sentence.

6.   Double space text and notes.

7.   Use only one side of the paper.

8.   Center main headings with subheadings flush with left margins.

9.   Number pages in upper left hand corner or in the center of the bottom of every page, with the exception of the first page.

10.   Type a title page with the name of the work and your name as author.

11.   For long direct quotes:

   (A).   All quotes should be indented one inch from left margin.
   (B).   If quote is over 100 words, single-space it.
   (C).   If quote is under 100 words, double-space it.
   (D).   Cite source for all quoted material.
To save space you may omit part of a quotation (be sure not to change meaning) by using three spaced periods ... (known as ellipsis marks). If used

at the end of a sentence or at the beginning of a sentence, use as stated. (i.e., "...John Doe was born in 1851...") Insert your own remarks in brackets (*i.e.*, "... John Doe was born in 1851..."). If inside the quotation there is another quotation, use single quotation marks.

If your project involves publication of a book, it is wise to consult several printers, book manufacturers, and genealogical publishers about their services. Each has a different function which may or may not be of help to you. Ask for an explanation of the printing process and the forms of printing. Be prepared to provide information concerning the number of copies needed and information on the resources available for the production of the book. The technical production of a book can become very involved.

If you are writing an article with the idea of submitting it to a particular publication, then, by all means, study other articles found in that publication. Write the editor for any specific instructions on submitting an article. Potential commercial writers will find of interest Anita Cheek Milner's "Professional Aspects of Writing Articles," <u>Association of Professional Genealogists Newsletter</u>, Vol. 3 (Nov. 1981), pp. 1-3.

SUGGESTED FORM FOR ARRANGEMENT OF A BOOK

Title Page (title, author, publisher, place of publication, date of publication, and copyright notice).

Dedication (Optional)

Table of Contents

Introduction, Preface, or Foreword (The last two deal with scope and/or purpose)

List of Illustrations

Text

Appendix (An Excursus may appear at the end of a chapter before notes if endnotes are used)

Bibliography

Index

Once your article or book is in print, you are likely to receive additional information. File it for the future. Be proud of your written work and repeat your feat. Write ANOTHER article or book... and WRITE IT RIGHT!

Appendix A

Purpose: Correlate,   analyze   and evaluate   research   resulting   from limited work.

OUTLINE

I. Introduction

   A. Purpose

   B. Results

   C. Recommendations

II. Philip Lewin

   A. Earliest Records

   B. Other Records

   C. Final Records involving descendants

PROGRESS REPORT ON THE LEWIN FAMILY OF MARYLAND

Philip Lewin of Prince George's County, Maryland, is an enigma. Why did he leave so many records but still remain so elusive? After some hours of research at the Hall of Records,

Annapolis, Maryland, information was gathered which documented three generations of the Lewin family of Prince George's County, Maryland. An analysis and evaluation of this information indicates that much pertinent data has been uncovered. This information has been used to construct the events in Philip Lewin's life from the mid 1680's to 1722. Research should be continued to attempt to locate any records that will shed additional light on Philip Lewin.

1. Philip Lewin (also spelled Lewen, Leweing, Lewing) was born ca. 1652-1662.[1] His approximate age can be calculated and estimated from his deposition and tax exemption.[2]

The earliest record discovered indicates that Philip Lewin had lived in Charles County, Maryland, prior to January 1686, when Thomas Jackson and Company sued Philip Lewin, Planter, late of Charles County, for £ 226 tobacco for trespass. The court awarded the plaintiffs £ 252 tobacco and occupation of the defendant's premises.[3]

He was in Ann Arundel County, Maryland, by 1692-1694.[4] In March 1697, he recorded his livestock mark: "A crop under bitt and hole x slitt out on the right ear and a cropp and hole on the left ear."[5]

On 16 December 1698, Philip Lewin purchased land in Prince George's County, Maryland, from Charles Calvert, Lord Baltimore, obtaining a tract containing one hundred six (106) acres called "Philip's Folly" bounded by a tract called "Dickinson's Delight" owned by Thomas Dickinson.[6] "Philip's Folly" was located on Tinkler/Tinkers branch adjoining a certain tract of land called "Dickinson's Delight" and laid out for one hundred six (106) acres.[7] He acquired an unknown interest in an unidentified tract which he mentioned in his will as being the land where his "grandson, Philip Gibbs' father now lives" (22 July 1722).[8] He also acquired a tract called "Stone Hill" by 22 July 1722.[9]

Philip Lewin witnessed a deed of John Accatamacca, Emperor of the Piscattaway (Indian tribe), to Colonel John Addison and William Hutchinson.[10] In 1713, Philip Lewin gave a deposition witnessed by Thomas Addison and John Bradford concerning "Piscattaway Manor" owned by James Neale, stating: "...about 18 or 20 years ago he and George Athoy came to a place on the South side of Piscattaway Creek about 150 yards below a landing place known by the name of Green Landing and Athoy said a white Oak was the boundary of James Neale's land called St. James."[11] At the time of this deposition, the

105

clerk failed to ask the age of Philip
Lewin, but the clerk later estimated it
to be about sixty years (11 Nov.
1712).[12]

In 1719, Philip Lewin was included
in a list of taxables for Piscattaway
Hundred, Prince George's County,
Maryland.[13] In March 1722, he was on
his petition setting forth great age,
exempted by court order from that
county to be "levey free" (tax exempt)
for the future.[14]

Philip Lewin wrote his will on 20
July 1722, and, less than one month
later, on 15 August 1722, it was
probated.[15] He mentioned real and
personal property that was to be given
to named children and grandchildren,
but no wife was mentioned.

Known Children of Philip Lewin, wife
unknown:[16]

+ 2. i. Elizabeth Lewin
+ 3. ii. Mary Lewin

2. Elizabeth Lewin was born ca. 1680-
1685. Her age can be estimated from
the birth of her first child,
Levin/Lewin Jones, born ca. 1701-05.[17]
She married first, Edward Jones, who
died in April or May 1722.[18] There
were five children by this marriage who
were alive at the time of their
father's death.[19]

106

By May 1723, Elizabeth Lewin Jones had married Henry Barnes.[20] He was dead by May 1727[21], survived by his widow, Elizabeth[22] and two children, Mary and Henry.[22] Elizabeth (Lewin Jones) Barnes last appears in the records as a taxable of Upper Piscattaway Hundred in 1733.[23]

Issue of Elizabeth Lewin, husband Edward Jones

4.   i.   Levin (or Lewin) Jones
5.   ii. James Jones
6.   iii. Edward Jones
7.   iv. William Jones
8.   v.   John Jones
9.   vi. Philip Jones

Issue of Elizabeth Lewin, husband Henry Barnes

10. vii. Mary Barnes
11. viii. Henry Barnes

3.   Mary Lewin was born ca. 1687 and died shortly before her father, Philip Lewin.[24] She was survived by her husband, James Gibbs, and six children.[25] James Gibbs died by March 1724/25,[26] the result of a drowning accident.[27]

Issue of Mary Lewin, husband James Gibbs

107

12.	i.	Philip Gibbs
13.	ii.	James Gibbs
14.	iii.	Mary Ann Gibbs
15.	iv.	Mary Gibbs
16.	v.	Andrew Gibbs
17.	vi.	Jane Gibbs

REFERENCE AND NOTES

[1]Estimated date of birth calculated considering all records. He would have been at least 21 years of age in 1686 when he was styled Planter, 35 to 48 years, in 1700 and at least 60-70 years of age by 1722. Using a birth year of 1652-1665, he would have become an adult by 1673-1686 and would have been 57-70 years of age at the time of his death in 1722. The higher figure is more probable and certainly reasonable from present records.

[2]"Deposition of Philip Lewin" (11 Nov. 1712), Maryland Chancery Court Record, #3(1712-1714), Liber PL, p. 44 (hereinafter cited "Deposition"), Hall of Records, Annapolis, Md. (hereinafter cited "HR"); Prince George's Co., MD (hereinafter cited "P.G. Co., Md.") Court Proceedings (1720-1722), Liber K, p. 488, HR.

[3]Charles County, Maryland, Court Records (1686-1688) Liber N pp. 253-254 (15 Jan. 1686), HR.

[4]Estimated from 1712 deposition

statement of events "18 to 20 years age" (1692-1694). See second citation N. 2, _supra_.

[5]P.G. Co., Md., Court Proceedings, Liber A, p.299, HR.

[6]Patent to Philip Lewing, P.G. Co., MD, Liber WD, pp. 220-221. (See also Patents, CC#4, p. 144), HR.

[7]"Will of Philip Lewin, " P.G. Co., Md., Will Book #17 (1721-1722) pp. 293-294 (hereinafter cited "Will of Philip Lewin"), HR.

[8]_Ibid._

[9]_Ibid._

[10]P.G. Co., Md., Deeds (1696-1702) Vol. A, p. 404, HR.

[11]"Deposition", N.2 _supra_.

[12]_Ibid._

[13]Manuscript Archives of Maryland, The Black Books, Vol. X, pp. 1-81, Proprietary Papers (1708-1785)... a list of taxables in Piscataway Hundred, taken by John Middleton, constable for the year 1719.

[14]P.G. Co., Md., Court Proceedings (1720-1722) Liber K, p. 488, HR.

[15] "Will of Philip Lewin," N.7, *supra*.

[16] *Ibid*.

[17] Piscataway or St. John's Parish, now called King George's Parish, Liber C, Baptisms, (1691-1800), pp. 8-93. Elizabeth Lewin's age can be estimated from the birth of her first child Levin or Lewin Jones ca. 1701-1705. He (Lewin Jones) made his mark, as the Nearest of Kin, to Philip Lewin's Inventory.

[18] "Will of Edward Jones," P.G. Co., Md., Will Book A&D #2 pp. 242-243 (18 April 1722-29 May 1722).

[19] "Philip Lewin--A Preliminary Study," "Bulletin," Prince George's County Genealogical Society, XI (April 1980) pp. 83-84.

[20] P.G. Co., Md., Accounts (1722-1724) pp. 173-174 (21 May 1723: Henry Barnes and Elizabeth, his wife, Executrix of all and singular the goods, chattels, and credits of Philip Lewin).

[21] P.G. Co., Md., Bonds, Box 6 folder 57 (2 May 1727: 400 Sterling bond on estate of Henry Barnes).

[22] P.G. Co., Md., Accounts (1728-1729) pp. 19-20 (30 Jan. 1727/28: heirs, Mary and Henry Barnes, eldest five years).

[23] Manuscript Archives of Maryland, The Black Books, Vol. II, No. 116 (1733) pp. 39-40.

[24] "Will of Philip Lewin," N.7, *supra*.

[25] "Philip Lewin--A Preliminary Study," N.19, *supra*.

[26] P.G. Co., Md., Testamentary Proceedings (1724-1727) No. 27, p. 165 (24 March 1724/25: Catherine Gibbs, widow and relict of James Gibbs...).

[27] P.G. Co., Md., Court Proceedings (Aug. 1726-Nov. 1727) Liber N, p. 119 (Nov. Ct. 1726: Catherine Gibbs by her petition sets forth that she lost her husband in a drowning accident and her infant child is devoid of human sense...).

Appendix B

PROOFREADERS' MARKS

∧ , insert at this point

, space or more space

[, carry farther to the left

] , carry farther to the right

|| , straighten end of lines

⊥ , push down a space which prints as a
mark

✕ , broken or imperfect type

¶ , make a new paragraph

[/] , brackets

(/) , parentheses

? , is this correct as set?--used in
the margin

wf, wrong front--used when a character
is of a wrong size or style

ital, put in italic type--used in
margin with __ under text matter

rom, put in roman type--used in the

margin with __ under text matter

dele, take out or expunge

bf, put in boldface type--used in margin with ˷˷˷ under the text matter

tr, transpose--used in the margin

lc, lowercase--used in the margin with a slanting line drawn through the letter in the text

sm caps, put in small capitals--double lines drawn under the letters or words

caps, put in capitals--triple lines drawn under the letters or word

ld, insert a lead between lines

stet, restore words crossed out-- usually written in the margin with dots under the words to be kept

awk, awkward sentence

dict, see your dictionary

frag, sentence fragment

gr, error in grammar

il, illegible writing

ms, error in manuscript form

nc, not clear

P, error in punctuation

R, rewrite page or portion indicated

ro, run-on sentence

sp, error in spelling

ss, error in sentence structure

t, error in tense

ww, wrong word

Appendix C

SOME COMMONLY USED ABBREVIATIONS

A, a,   acre or acres
acct,   account
admr,   administrator or administratrix
ae, aet,   age or aged
A.G., Accredited Genealogist
A.D.S., autograph document signed
a.k.a., also known as
alias,   an assumed name, or the married
(or maiden) name of a woman
A.L.S., autograph letter signed
anon., anonymous
ante, before, or prior to
anti, against
app., appendix
A.R. (Anno Regni), the year of the
reign of
assn., association
B.A., Bachelor of Arts
b., born
bap., baptized
bef, before
bet, between
bibliog., bibliography
Bk. (Bks. plural), book(s)
B.L. Wt., Bounty Land Warrant
bp, baptized
b pl, birthplace
bro, brother
bro/o, brother of
B.S., bill of sale
ca. (circa), about

C.A.L.S., Certified American Lineage Specialist
cert, certificate or certified
C.G., Certified Genealogist
C.G.R.S., Certified Genealogical Record Searcher
cf. (*confer*), compare
ch., chapter
chr, christened
co., county
col., column
comp. (comps. plural), compiler(s)
d., died
dau., daughter
D.B., deed book
dec, dec'd, deceased
d/o, da/o, dau/o, daughter of
do (*ditto*), the same
D. of G., D.G., deed of gift
D. of T., D.T., deed of trust
dept., department
diss., dissertation
doc. (docs. plural), document(s)
d.s.p. (*decessit sine prole*), died without issue
d.s.p.m. (*decessit sine prole mascula*), died without male issue
d.s.p.s. (*decessit sine prole supersite*), died without surviving issue
d.v.m. (*decessit vita matris*), died in the mother's lifetime
d.v.p. (*decessit vita patris*), died in the father's lifetime
e.g. (*exempli gratia*), for example
ed. cit. (*editio citata*), edition cited
ed. (eds. plural), editor(s)

esp., especially
Esq, esquire
est., estate
et al (et alii), and others
etc., (et cetera), and so forth
et ux (et uxor), and wife
exec., executor
F.A.S.G., Fellow American Society of Genealogists
f, female
f, fa, father
f, ff, following page or pages
facs. (or facsim.), facsimile
fig., figure
fn., footnote
F.N.G.S., Fellow, National Genealogical Society
f/o, fa/o, father of
fol., (fols. plural), folio(s)
gdn, guardian
Gent, gentleman
gr, grant or granted, grantor or grantee
h, heir
h, husband
hic jacet, here lies
hic sit (hic situs), here is buried
hist., history or historian
h/o, husband of
H.S. (hic sepultus), here is buried
Hun., Hundred
i.e. (id est), that is
ibid. (ibidem), in the same place
imp (imprimis), in the first place
in esse, in being, usually refers to an unborn child
inf, infant

infra., below
int, intestate
int, interest
int, interred
inst (Instant), within the same month
introd., introduction
ills., illustrated or illustrator
jour., journal
J.P., Justice of the Peace
jur, jury or juror
jur, jurat
l., line
l, lived
L (libra), pound
L.G.O., Land Grant Office
lib. (liber), book
lic., license
loc. cit. (loco citato), in the place cited
L.S. (locus sigilii), the place of the seal
L.s.d., Pounds, shillings, pence
m, mar, married
m, man or male
m, mother
MS. (MSS plural), manuscript(s)
M. A., Master of Arts
M. G., Minister of the Gospel
M. M., Monthly Meeting (Quaker)
M. S., Master of Science
misc., miscellaneous
Mr., Mister or Master
Mrs., Mistress: an unmarried woman of high social standing, or a married woman's title
N., (NN. plural), note(s)
N. B. (nota bene), take notice

N.d., no date
N.n., no name
N.p., no place
N. pag., no pagination
N. pub., no publisher
next friend, one acting legally for another
no., number
nr, near
N. S., New Style (Gregorian calendar)
nunc, nuncapative, spoken, an oral will
ob (obit), died
op. (opus), work
op. cit. (opere citato), in the work cited
O. S., Old Style (calendar)
p. (pp. plural), page(s)
P. A., power of attorney
par., paragraph
passim, here and there
pat, paternal
per, by means of
Ph.D., Doctor of Philosophy
pltf, plaintiff
P. R., probate record
pr, prob, probate or probated
pref., preface
pt. (pts. plural), part(s)
pvd, proved
q.v. (quod vide), which see
R., Range (legal land description)
R.G., Record Group
rev., revised
R.I.P. (requiescat in pace), rest in peace
rpt., reprint
s, son

s, shilling
s.p. (sine prole), without issue
s.p.s. (sine prole supersite), without
surviving issue
sec., section
ser., series
sic, thus
sine die, without date
s/o, son of
soc., society
supra, above
T., Township (legal land description)
t, temp (tempore), in the time of
trans., translator
ult (ultimo), in the month immediately
preceding
ux (uxor), wife
V. (verso), the back (of a page)
v (versus), against
v (vidi), see
v.d., various dates
V.O.M. (Voluns Deus Minister), minister
by the will of God
V.R., vital record
viz. (videlicet), namely
vol. (vols. plural), volume(s)
vs (versus), against
w, wife or widow
w/, with
W.B., will book
wid, widr, widow or widower
w/o, wife of
w/o, without
Y.M., Yearly Meeting (Quaker)
yr., year

INDEX

ORDER FORM

D.R. Barnes Associates
Box 5755
Rockville, MD 20055-0755

Please send _____ number of copies at $7.95 plus
$1.00 for postage and handling to:

Name _____

Address _____

State_____

Zip _____

(Maryland residents add 5% sales tax)

*Libraries/book dealers write for information for bulk
purchases.*

ORDER FORM

D.R. Barnes Associates
Box 5755
Rockville, MD 20055-0755

Please send _____ number of copies at $7.95 plus
$1.00 for postage and handling to:

Name _____

Address _____

State_____

Zip _____

(Maryland residents add 5% sales tax)

*Libraries/book dealers write for information for bulk
purchases.*

ORDER FORM

D.R. Barnes Associates
Box 5755
Rockville, MD 20055-0755

Please send _____ number of copies at $7.95 plus
$1.00 for postage and handling to:

Name _____

Address _____

State_____

Zip _____

(Maryland residents add 5% sales tax)

Libraries/book dealers write for information for bulk purchases.